THE AGE OF INNOCENCE

For the rich and the fashionable, New York society in the 1870s was a world full of rules: rules about when to wear a black tie, or the correct time to pay an afternoon visit; rules about who you could invite to your evening parties or sit next to at the opera; rules about who was an acceptable person, and who was not.

Countess Ellen Olenska, who has lived for many years in Europe as the wife of a Polish Count, returns alone to her family in New York. She hopes to leave the pain of her unhappy marriage behind her, but she does not understand the rules of New York society. Newland Archer, however, understands them only too well, and the girl he is engaged to marry, young May Welland, lives her life by the rules, because she cannot imagine any other way of living.

Newland, May, and Ellen are caught in a battle between love, honour, and duty – a battle where strong feelings hide behind polite smiles, where much is left unsaid, and where a single expressive look across a crowded room can carry more meaning than a hundred words.

OXFORD BOOKWORMS LIBRARY
Classics

The Age of Innocence
Stage 5 (1800 headwords)

Series Editor: Jennifer Bassett
Founder Editor: Tricia Hedge
Activities Editors: Jennifer Bassett and Christine Lindop

EDITH WHARTON

The Age of Innocence

Retold by
Clare West

OXFORD UNIVERSITY PRESS

OXFORD

UNIVERSITY PRESS

Great Clarendon Street, Oxford OX2 6DP

Oxford University Press is a department of the University of Oxford.
It furthers the University's objective of excellence in research, scholarship,
and education by publishing worldwide in

Oxford New York

Auckland Cape Town Dar es Salaam Hong Kong Karachi
Kuala Lumpur Madrid Melbourne Mexico City Nairobi
New Delhi Shanghai Taipei Toronto

With offices in

Argentina Austria Brazil Chile Czech Republic France Greece
Guatemala Hungary Italy Japan Poland Portugal Singapore
South Korea Switzerland Thailand Turkey Ukraine Vietnam

OXFORD and OXFORD ENGLISH are registered trade marks of
Oxford University Press in the UK and in certain other countries

ISBN 978 0 19 479216 5

A complete recording of this Bookworms edition of
The Age of Innocence is available.

Printed in China

acknowledgements
Illustrated by: Gavin Reece

Word count (main text): 24,820 words

For more information on the Oxford Bookworms Library,
visit www.oup.com/elt/bookworms

CONTENTS

STORY INTRODUCTION i

PEOPLE IN THIS STORY viii

1 A stranger in New York 1

2 Newland has doubts 11

3 The Countess causes trouble 21

4 A second visit to the Countess 30

5 May surprises Newland 38

6 The wedding and beyond 50

7 Newland in Boston 58

8 The Beaufort scandal 67

9 Ellen returns to New York 74

10 Newland visits Paris 85

GLOSSARY 91

ACTIVITIES: Before Reading 94

ACTIVITIES: While Reading 95

ACTIVITIES: After Reading 97

ABOUT THE AUTHOR 101

ABOUT THE BOOKWORMS LIBRARY 102

PEOPLE IN THIS STORY

Newland Archer's family
Newland Archer
Janey Archer, *Newland's sister*
Adeline Archer, *Newland's mother*
Louisa van der Luyden, *Adeline's cousin*
Henry van der Luyden, *Louisa's husband*
the Misses du Lac, *Newland's aunts*
the Duke of St Austrey, *Louisa's English cousin*

May Welland's family
May Welland
Mr Welland, *May's father*
Mrs Welland, *May's mother*
Countess Ellen Olenska, *May's cousin*
Count Olenski, *Ellen Olenska's husband*
Mrs Manson Mingott, *grandmother to May and Ellen*
Medora Manson, *Ellen's aunt*
Mr Lovell Mingott, *uncle to May and Ellen*
Mrs Lovell Mingott, *Mr Mingott's wife*
Regina Beaufort, *niece to Mrs Manson Mingott*
Julius Beaufort, *Regina's husband*

Other people in the story
Lawrence Lefferts } *New Yorkers,*
Sillerton Jackson } *and friends of Newland Archer*
Sophy Jackson, *Sillerton Jackson's sister*
Mrs Lemuel Struthers, *a friend of Julius Beaufort*
Monsieur Rivière, *Count Olenski's French secretary*
Mr Letterblair, *a lawyer, and Newland Archer's employer*
the Carfrys, *English friends of Mrs Archer*
the Blenkers, *friends of Ellen Olenska*
Fanny Ring, *Julius Beaufort's mistress, later wife*
Dallas, Mary, and Bill Archer, *Newland Archer's children*
Fanny Beaufort, *daughter of Julius Beaufort and Fanny Ring*

CHAPTER 1

A STRANGER IN NEW YORK

When Newland Archer arrived at the New York Academy of Music, one January evening in the early 1870s, the opera had already begun. There was no reason why the young man should not have come earlier. He had had dinner at seven, alone with his mother and sister, and then sat unhurriedly smoking his cigar in his private library. But fashionable young men did not arrive early at the opera. That was one of the unwritten rules of society, and in Newland Archer's New York these rules were as important as life and death.

Another reason for the young man's delay was that he enjoyed looking forward to pleasures just as much as actually experiencing them, and Gounod's *Faust* was one of his favourite operas. As he opened the door at the back of his box, he felt he had chosen just the right moment to arrive. Christine Nilsson, the Swedish singer whom all New York had gathered to hear, was singing, 'He loves me – he loves me not – *he loves me*!'

She sang in Italian, of course, not in English, since an unquestioned law of the musical world demanded that the German words of French operas sung by Swedish singers should be translated into Italian, for the clearer understanding of English-speaking audiences. This seemed as natural to Newland as all the other laws that governed his life, like never appearing in society without a flower in his buttonhole, and having two silver-backed brushes for his hair.

He turned his eyes away from the singer and looked at the audience. Directly opposite him was the box of old Mrs Manson Mingott, who was now so fat that she was unable to attend the opera, but whose family often came on fashionable nights. Tonight the front of the box was filled by her daughter-in-law, Mrs Lovell Mingott, and her daughter, Mrs Welland. A little behind these ladies in their heavy silks sat a young girl in white, with her eyes fixed on the singer. As Madame Nilsson's voice rose above the silent audience (the boxes always stopped talking during this song), a warm pink spread over the girl's face and shoulders, right down to the top of her evening dress. She dropped her eyes to the enormous bunch of white flowers on her knee, and touched them gently.

Newland recognized his gift to her, and was pleased. 'The dear girl!' he thought. 'She has no idea what this opera is all about.' He watched her face, thinking fondly of her simple innocence. It would be his manly duty and pleasure to educate her. 'We'll read all the great books together, by the Italian Lakes . . .'

It was only that afternoon that May Welland had let him know she 'cared' (the word that nice New York girls used to confess their love). Already his imagination, jumping ahead of the engagement ring, the first kiss, and the wedding, showed her at his side, sharing his interests as they travelled round the ancient places of Europe together.

He did not want the future Mrs Newland Archer to remain a simple, innocent girl. He intended that, with his help, she would become a social success among the married women of his circle, confident in any situation, always able to make clever and amusing conversation. If he had looked deep within himself (as he sometimes nearly did), he would have found there the wish that his wife should have the same social experience and eagerness to please as the married lady whose company he had enjoyed for two quite pleasant years.

How this wonderful being of fire and ice was to be created, he had never taken the time to consider. He knew his views on women were shared by all the carefully dressed, buttonhole-flowered men who greeted him from their boxes or visited him in his own, and he did not see a need to think differently.

'My God!' said Lawrence Lefferts suddenly. He was one of the group of Newland's friends in the box – a man who knew more about 'form' than anyone else in New York. He always knew what was, or was not, socially correct behaviour, and he always had the answers to all the mysterious questions, such as when a black tie should or should not be worn.

'Look!' he added, handing his opera-glasses to his old friend Sillerton Jackson, who was standing next to him.

Newland saw with surprise that a new figure had entered old Mrs Mingott's box. It was that of a young woman, a little less tall than May Welland, with curly brown hair and a dark blue, unusually low-cut evening dress. Sillerton Jackson returned the opera-glasses to Lawrence Lefferts, and the young men in the box waited eagerly to hear what old Mr Jackson had to say, since he knew as much about 'family' as Mr Lefferts knew about 'form'. He also knew the details of all the scandals and mysteries that had lain under New York's calm surface for the last fifty years. There was a moment's silence. Then Sillerton Jackson said simply, 'I didn't think the Mingotts would have attempted that.' Newland felt annoyed that the box which was the centre of attention for so many men was the one in which his fiancée was sitting, and he could not at first imagine why the newcomer was creating such excitement. Then he remembered who she was, and immediately felt even more annoyed. No, indeed, no one would have thought the Mingotts would have attempted that!

He was in no doubt that the young woman was May Welland's cousin, whom the family always spoke of as 'poor Ellen Olenska'. He knew that she had suddenly arrived from Europe a day or two previously, and he had heard from May that she herself had been to see poor Ellen, who was staying with her grandmother, old Mrs Mingott. There was nothing mean or ungenerous in the young man's heart, and he was glad that his future wife was being kind (in private) to her unhappy cousin. But to welcome Countess Olenska into the family circle was a very different thing from producing her in society, at the opera, of all places, and in the very box with the young girl whose engagement to him, Newland Archer, was to be announced within a few weeks.

Of course, he knew that old Mrs Mingott was as socially daring as any man in New York. In spite of having no beauty or family connections, she had made an excellent marriage when quite young, and had become extremely wealthy when her husband died. Since then she had done exactly what she wanted, and made sure that all her children and grandchildren, not to mention half of New York, obeyed her orders.

As he was thinking, Newland suddenly became aware of the conversation going on around him in his box.

'After all,' a young man was saying, 'just *what* happened?'

'Well – she left him. Nobody tries to say she didn't,' someone replied.

'But her husband, this Polish Count,' said the young man, 'he's an awful man, isn't he?'

'The very worst type,' said Lawrence Lefferts. 'I knew him in

France. Rather handsome. When he isn't with women, he collects paintings. Pays any price for both, I understand.'

There was a general laugh. Lefferts continued, 'Anyway, she ran off with his secretary. It didn't last long. I believe her uncle, Lovell Mingott, went to bring her back – she was living alone in Venice. He said she was desperately unhappy. That's all right – but bringing her to the opera's another thing.'

'It's strange that they've brought Miss Welland along as well,' whispered someone, with a sideways look at Newland.

'Oh, she's here on Grandmother's orders, no doubt,' Lefferts laughed. 'The old lady has doubtless demanded the whole family's support for the Countess.'

Suddenly Newland felt he must be seen by his fiancée's side, to inform the waiting world of his engagement to May Welland, and to help her through any difficulties caused by her cousin's situation. He left his box and hurried round to old Mrs Mingott's. As he entered, his eyes met May's, and he saw she had immediately understood his reason for coming. People in their social circle never expressed their feelings in free and open discussion, and the fact that she and he understood each other without a word seemed, to the young man, to bring them closer than any explanation would have done. Her eyes said, 'You see why I am here,' and his answered, 'I would not for the world have wanted you to stay away.'

'You know my niece, Countess Olenska?' Mrs Welland asked as she shook hands with her future son-in-law.

Newland greeted Ellen Olenska politely, and then sat down beside May. In a low voice he said, 'I hope you've told Madame Olenska that we're engaged? I want everybody to know – I want you to announce it this evening at the ball.'

May's face turned pink, and she looked at him with shining eyes. 'If you can persuade Mother,' she said, 'but why change the date we agreed for the announcement?' She saw his answer in his eyes and added, smiling confidently now, 'Tell my cousin

Newland rose and seated himself at Countess Olenska's side.

6

yourself – I give you permission. She says you used to play together when you were children.'

She made way for him by pushing back her chair, and Newland rose and seated himself at Countess Olenska's side.

'We *did* use to play together, didn't we?' the Countess asked, turning her serious eyes to his. 'You were a bad boy, and kissed me once behind a door.' She looked out over the audience. 'Ah, how this brings my childhood back to me – I see everybody here in short trousers and pretty little dresses,' she added in her almost foreign accent, her eyes returning to his face.

The young man was shocked that she should make jokes about New York's most important people, who were, at this moment, passing judgement on her. He answered a little stiffly, 'Yes, you have been away a very long time.'

'Oh, centuries and centuries,' she said, 'so long that I'm sure I'm dead and buried, and this dear old place is heaven.'

And this, for reasons Newland could not explain, seemed an even less polite way of describing New York society.

That night most of New York was expected to attend the Beauforts' ball. The Beauforts were one of the few families to own a house with a ballroom, and this fact helped New Yorkers to forget certain uncomfortable things about Julius Beaufort. The question was, who *was* Beaufort? He had arrived from nowhere to build up a fortune for himself in banking, but he was a man with bad habits, a bitter tongue and a mysterious past. Regina Beaufort, indeed, belonged to one of America's oldest families. As a penniless young beauty, she had been introduced to New York society by her cousin, Medora Manson, and had made what people thought was a most foolish marriage to Julius Beaufort.

Foolish or not, only two years after her marriage, it was agreed that her house was the most luxurious and comfortable in New York. Growing younger and blonder and more beautiful each year, she was the queen of Beaufort's palace, and drew all the world there without lifting her jewelled little finger. Some people whispered that it was Beaufort himself who trained all the servants, taught the cook new dishes, chose the plants for the gardens, and invited the guests. But to the world he gave the appearance of a carefree man of wealth, who just happened to be present at his wife's brilliant parties.

Newland Archer arrived a little late at the ball, as fashionable young men usually did. He had been thinking hard during his walk from the opera. Now he was beginning to fear that the Mingotts might go too far – that, in fact, they might be under old Grandmother Mingott's orders to bring Countess Olenska to the ball. That, thought Archer, would be a serious mistake.

As he entered the ballroom, he could see Mrs Welland and her daughter standing opposite him. Surrounding May Welland was a small group of young men and girls, and from the handshaking, laughing and smiles, it was clear that she had announced her engagement. Newland paused a moment. He had wanted the announcement to be made, but he would have preferred it to be done at a quieter time, not in the heat and noise of a crowded ballroom. He was glad to see that May shared this feeling. Her eyes met his and their look said, 'Remember, we're doing this because it's right.'

He made his way towards her, and after receiving warm congratulations from many of the group, he drew his fiancée into the middle of the dance floor and put his arm around her waist. 'Now we won't have to talk,' he said, smiling into her clear eyes, as they started dancing. She made no answer, but her lips trembled into a smile. 'Dear,' whispered Newland, pressing her to him. What a new life it was going to be, with this whiteness, this beauty, this goodness at his side!

When the dance was over, the couple sat down in a quiet corner, and Newland pressed her hand to his lips.

'You see, I made the announcement, as you asked me to,' she said.

'Yes, I couldn't wait,' he answered, smiling. 'Only I wish it didn't have to be at a ball.'

'Yes, I know.' She looked at him intelligently. 'But after all, even here we're alone together, aren't we?'

'Oh, dearest – always!' Newland cried.

Clearly she was always going to understand, she was always going to say the right thing. He continued happily, 'The worst of it is that I want to kiss you and I can't.' But looking quickly round, he could see there was no one nearby, and so he placed a kiss lightly on her lips. She sat silent, and the world lay like a sunlit valley at their feet.

'Did you tell my cousin Ellen?' she asked a moment later, in a dream-like voice.

He remembered that he had not wanted to speak of such things to the strange foreign woman, and had to lie. 'I didn't have the chance in the end.'

'Ah.' She looked disappointed, but continued, 'You must, because I didn't either. She's been away so long that she's rather sensitive, and might feel hurt if we didn't tell her.'

Newland looked at her lovingly. 'Dearest! Of course I'll tell her.' He looked anxiously towards the crowded ballroom. 'But I haven't seen her yet. Has she come?'

'No, at the last minute she decided her dress wasn't good enough for a ball, so she didn't come.'

'Oh, well,' said Newland, secretly delighted. Nothing about his fiancée pleased him more than her determination not to see anything unpleasant, like the real reason for her cousin's absence.

During the next day Newland and May, with May's mother, paid their first social visits as an engaged couple. At old Mrs Mingott's house, they discovered that Countess Olenska was out. But just as their visit came to an end and they were preparing to leave, she returned, followed by the unexpected figure of Julius Beaufort. And in the hall, while May and her mother were putting on their coats, Newland realized that the Countess was looking at him with a questioning smile.

'Of course you know already – about May and me,' he said to her, with a shy laugh. 'I meant to tell you last night.'

The smile passed from Countess Olenska's eyes to her lips; she looked younger, more like the playful Ellen Mingott of his boyhood. 'Of course I know, yes. And I'm so glad.' She held out her hand. 'Goodbye. Come and see me some day,' she added, still looking at Newland.

On their way home, none of them mentioned Ellen Olenska, but Newland knew Mrs Welland was thinking, 'It's a mistake for Ellen to be seen, so soon after her arrival, with Julius Beaufort.' The young man himself was thinking, 'And she ought to know that an engaged man doesn't spend his time visiting married women. But perhaps that's acceptable in the circles she's been moving in.' He thanked heaven he was a New Yorker, and about to marry one of his own kind.

CHAPTER 2

NEWLAND HAS DOUBTS

The next evening old Mr Sillerton Jackson came to have dinner with the Archers. Newland's mother, Adeline Archer, had long been a widow, and did not often go into society, but she liked to be well informed about what was going on. Her old friend Sillerton Jackson used to study people's lives with a collector's patience and a scientist's attention to detail. So whenever anything happened that Mrs Archer wished to know about, she asked Mr Jackson to dinner.

In a perfect world, Mr Jackson would have hoped for Mrs Archer's food to be a little better. But after all, you couldn't have everything. If you had dinner with the Mansons or the Lovell Mingotts, who cared about eating and clothes and money, you ate the finest food and drank the best wines. On the other hand, if you were invited by the Archers or the van der Luydens, who had no time for the coarser kinds of pleasure, you could talk about the Swiss Alps and the most recent books. So when a friendly command came from Mrs Archer, Mr Jackson, who liked to find the best in every situation, would say to his sister Sophy, 'I over-ate last time I went to Mrs Mingott's – it'll do me good to eat a bit less at Adeline's.'

Mrs Archer and her unmarried daughter Janey lived on the ground floor of the family house, while Newland had the whole of the first floor to himself. Mother and daughter spent all their time together, reading or sewing in their beautifully furnished sitting room, or occasionally travelling, in search of the scenery or works of art they both admired so much. The long habit of living together in such closeness had given them similar interests, the same vocabulary, and even the same way of beginning a sentence with 'Mother thinks' or 'Janey thinks', when each of them wanted to give an opinion that was, in fact, their own.

They looked almost like sisters, both tall, pale, and a little round shouldered, with long noses and sweet smiles. As the years passed, however, Mrs Archer's black silks were stretched more tightly round her thickening waist, while Miss Archer's brown and purple dresses hung more loosely on her virgin figure.

Mother and daughter loved each other deeply, and admired and respected Newland. This admiration secretly pleased him, and he loved them for it; he considered it a good thing for a man to be respected and obeyed in his own house.

Newland had his own reasons for staying at home that evening. He knew old Jackson would talk about Ellen Olenska, and of course Mrs Archer and Janey wanted to hear what he had to tell. All three would be a little embarrassed by Newland's presence, now that his future connection to the Mingott family had been announced, and the young man waited with amused curiosity to see what effect this would have on their conversation.

Mrs Archer began indirectly, by talking about Mrs Struthers, a guest whom New York society had been surprised to see at the Beauforts' ball. 'It's a pity she was invited,' she said gently, 'but Julius Beaufort insisted, I hear.'

'Beaufort will never understand what is and is not acceptable,' said Mr Jackson, cautiously inspecting the fish, and wondering for the thousandth time why Mrs Archer's cook always burnt it.

'Oh, of course Beaufort is not a gentleman,' said Mrs Archer. 'And Mrs Struthers is . . .' She looked briefly at Janey and paused. There were facts that were not suitable for an unmarried woman to know – or at least, to discuss in public.

'Mrs Struthers is a woman who once lived as a—' Mr Jackson, catching sight of Janey, whose eyes were wide with interest, stopped, then went on, 'Until Lemuel Struthers came along, and – in the end – married her.' He left a little pause before and after the words 'in the end', and the pauses were full of meaning.

'Oh well, so many people behave badly nowadays, it doesn't matter,' said Mrs Archer carelessly. In fact, the ladies were not interested in Mrs Struthers, and Mrs Archer chose the moment to ask what she and Janey really wanted to know. 'And Newland's new cousin – Countess Olenska? Was *she* at the ball too?'

Adeline Archer had been very glad to hear of her son's engagement. Young men could do such unexpected, foolish things, and some women would do anything to trap a husband. But Newland had made an excellent choice – May Welland was one of the wealthiest and most beautiful girls in New York, and from a highly respected family. Mrs Archer felt that now she could relax, confident that her only son would live in safe and blameless domesticity for the rest of his life.

However, she thought it was a little unfortunate that his engagement meant he would be related to Madame Olenska, who seemed to have forgotten, if indeed she had ever understood, the importance of following society's rules at all times.

Mr Jackson leaned back in his chair. 'No, she was *not* at the ball,' he said heavily and deliberately.

'Perhaps the Beauforts don't know her,' Janey suggested,

looking innocent, though she knew very well that was not true.

'Mrs Beaufort may not, but Beaufort certainly does,' replied Mr Jackson. 'Madame Olenska was seen walking up Fifth Avenue this afternoon with him by the whole of New York.'

'Oh dear!' cried Mrs Archer. 'How could she!'

Janey said, greatly daring, 'I heard she had on a dark blue dress at the opera, perfectly plain and flat – like a night-dress.'

'Janey!' said her mother, shocked, and Janey Archer blushed. 'Anyway,' continued Mrs Archer, 'she showed better taste in not going to the ball.'

'I don't think it was a question of good taste,' said Newland, wanting to annoy his mother a little. 'May said Ellen intended to go, and then decided her dress wasn't good enough.'

Mrs Archer smiled, pleased to learn her guess was correct. 'Poor Ellen! We must remember how strangely she was brought up by Medora Manson. What can you expect of a girl who was allowed to wear black silk at her very first evening ball?'

Newland suddenly became argumentative. 'She's "poor Ellen" certainly, because she had the bad luck to make a miserable marriage, but I don't see what she has to be ashamed of.'

'People do say that she . . .' began Mr Jackson, and stopped, looking at Janey again.

'Oh, I know!' cried Newland. 'They say the secretary helped her to get away from her cruel husband, who kept her more or less a prisoner. Well, what's wrong with that? Which man wouldn't offer his help in a case like that?'

'I hear she intends to get a divorce,' said Janey bravely.

'I hope she will!' cried Newland.

The word 'divorce' fell like a bomb in the calm purity of the Archer dining room. Mrs Archer gave her son a meaningful look, and the young man, conscious of the bad taste of discussing such personal matters in front of the servants, quickly changed the subject.

After dinner, as was the custom, the ladies went up to the sitting room, while Newland took his guest to the library. As Mr Jackson sat down in a comfortable armchair and happily lit one of Newland's excellent cigars, he said, 'You think the secretary just helped her to get away, my dear Newland? Well, he was still helping her a year later then, because someone met them living in Switzerland together.'

Newland reddened. 'Living together? Well, why not? Why shouldn't she start a new life? I hate the idea that a woman of her age should bury herself alive if her husband chooses to live

'Which man wouldn't offer his help in a case like that?' cried Newland.

with other women.' He turned away angrily to light his cigar. 'Women ought to be free, as free as we are,' he added, too irritated to realize the full meaning of his discovery.

Mr Sillerton Jackson stretched his feet closer to the fire and whistled in amusement. 'Really, Newland?' he said, with a smile. 'Well, it seems Count Olenski shares your view, because I don't think he's lifted a finger to get his wife back.'

That evening, after Mr Jackson's departure, Newland sat at his desk in the library, looking at the large photograph of May Welland which she had given him. With a new sense of fear he looked at the serious eyes and smiling, innocent mouth of the young creature who would soon be his responsibility. She was the terrifying product of the society he belonged to and believed in – a young girl who knew nothing and expected everything. Suddenly she seemed like a stranger, and he began to realize that marriage was not the safe harbour he had been taught to expect, but a voyage into unexplored seas.

The arrival of the Countess Olenska had disturbed him, and made him unsure of what was right, for the first time in his well-ordered life. Naturally, he would be a far kinder and more sensitive husband to May than Count Olenski had been to Ellen. But clearly, things could still go wrong in his marriage to May. What could he and she really know of each other, since it was his duty to hide his past from her, and her duty, as a marriageable girl, to have no past to hide? What if they should tire of each other, or annoy each other? He thought about his friends' marriages, and saw none that offered the loving friendship which he had been hoping for with May.

He was sincerely in love, and he knew that doubts were common in young men who were going to be married. He blamed Countess Olenska. Here he was, recently engaged – a moment for pure thoughts and cloudless hopes – and involved in a scandal which could bring all the kinds of problem he would much rather avoid.

A few days later the scandal worsened. The Lovell Mingotts, led by old Mrs Manson Mingott, had sent out cards inviting a number of guests to a dinner. The invitations were headed with the words, 'To meet the Countess Olenska'. Forty-eight hours later, the unbelievable had happened: everyone except the Beauforts and Sillerton Jackson had refused the Mingotts' invitation. It was clear that New York society had decided not to meet the Countess Olenska.

When Newland heard of this, he was extremely angry, and persuaded his mother to ask her influential cousin, Louisa van der Luyden, for her support.

The New York of Newland Archer's day was broadly made up of three groups of people. At the bottom were the respectable, ordinary families like the Leffertses or the Jacksons. Above them were the wealthy people of good family like the Mingotts and the Archers. And right at the top were just three families, the Dagonets, the Lannings, and the van der Luydens, all of whom were related to high-born European families.

Mrs Archer and Newland drove straight to the van der Luydens' large dark house in Madison Avenue. Here Louisa received them in her high-ceilinged sitting room full of solid, old-fashioned furniture, and listened politely to Mrs Archer's story. Her usual answer to any request for help was, 'I shall first have to talk this over with my husband,' but this time she rang for a servant and told him, 'If Mr van der Luyden has finished reading the newspaper, please ask him to be kind enough to come.'

In a few minutes Henry van der Luyden entered the room. He greeted Mrs Archer and congratulated Newland on his engagement. Then he listened quietly as Mrs Archer repeated what she had told his wife. There was a silence while the two almost royal figures considered the situation, the weight of social responsibility lying heavily on their thin, elderly shoulders. Newland and his mother waited respectfully.

Finally Henry van der Luyden spoke. 'As long as a member of a well-known family is supported by that family, their decision should be considered final. I had no idea that people were starting to behave so badly.' He looked at his wife, who bent her head in agreement. 'Newland, you may be aware that Louisa's English cousin, the Duke of St Austrey, is coming to stay with us for a few days. We are inviting a few friends to dinner here, to meet him, and I am sure Louisa will be as glad as I am if Countess Olenska will let us include her among our guests.'

'Thank you so much, Henry—' Mrs Archer began.

'There is nothing to thank me for, dear Adeline. This kind of thing must not happen in New York, and shall not, as long as I can prevent it.' And he guided his guests towards the door.

Two hours later everyone knew that the most respected couple in New York had invited Madame Olenska to dinner the following week, to meet their relation, the Duke of St Austrey.

It was generally agreed in New York that Countess Olenska had 'lost her looks'. She had been a brilliantly pretty child, who was adopted by her aunt, Medora Manson, after both her parents died young. Poor Medora married three unsuitable husbands, one after the other, and was widowed three times. However, she brought up Ellen as well as she could. They travelled constantly, and it was while travelling in Europe that Ellen met and married Count Olenski. When the marriage ended in disaster, she had returned to her relations in New York, to rest and to forget.

When Newland saw her enter the van der Luydens' dining room on the evening of the dinner, he disagreed at once with the general opinion of her appearance. She was paler and thinner than when she was younger, but there was a mysterious beauty about her – a sureness in the way she carried her head, an unspoken experience of suffering that lay behind those intelligent eyes. She was the youngest woman present, but the smooth soft faces of the older women seemed almost childlike compared with hers. It frightened Newland to think what had happened to her, to give her eyes like that.

When the men joined the ladies after dinner, the Duke went straight up to the Countess and they talked together like old friends. It was clear she had met him on her travels in Europe. At the end of their conversation, instead of waiting for another gentleman to come and talk to her, which was the custom in New York, she got up and came to sit beside Newland.

'May is a dear girl – so handsome and intelligent,' she said, smiling at him. 'Are you very much in love with her?'

Newland reddened, laughing. 'As much as a man can be.'

'How delightful! And you discovered each other yourselves – it wasn't arranged for you in any way?'

Newland looked at her in disbelief, and asked with a smile. 'Have you forgotten that in our country we don't allow our marriages to be arranged for us?'

She blushed, and at once he was sorry for his careless remark.

'Yes, I'd forgotten. You must forgive me if I sometimes make these mistakes. Things were so different, so bad, where I've come from.' She looked down and he saw that her lips trembled.

'I'm so sorry,' he said quickly, 'but you *are* among friends here, you know.'

'Yes, I know. Wherever I go, I have that feeling. That's why I came home. I want to forget everything in my recent past, to become a complete American again, like the Mingotts and the Wellands. Ah, here's May arriving, and you will want to hurry away to her,' she added, but without moving. Her eyes turned back from the door to rest on the young man's face.

The after-dinner guests were now entering the room, and Newland saw May with her mother. 'Oh, she's surrounded by people. She's being introduced to the Duke just now,' he said.

'Then stay with me a little longer,' Madame Olenska said in a low voice, just touching his knee with her finger. It was the lightest touch, but to him it was as exciting as a kiss.

'Yes, let me stay,' he whispered. But just then Mr van der Luyden came up, with a guest who wanted to meet the Countess, so Newland had to give up his seat.

Madame Olenska held out her hand to him, to say goodbye. 'Tomorrow, then, after five – I shall expect you,' she said.

'Tomorrow . . .' Newland heard himself repeating, although they had made no arrangement during their conversation.

As he moved away, he saw, waiting to meet the Countess, a number of the couples who had refused to meet her at the Lovell Mingotts', and it proved to him yet again the great influence that the van der Luydens had on New York society.

CHAPTER 3
THE COUNTESS CAUSES TROUBLE

The Countess had said, 'After five,' and at half past five the next day Newland was ringing the bell of her house in West Twenty-third Street. She had rented it from her aunt Medora, who was travelling again, but it was a strange area to live in – a narrow street of poor-looking houses which needed painting, a street inhabited by dressmakers and writers.

'The Count must have robbed her of her fortune as well as her dreams,' Newland thought as he looked around him.

The young man had not had an enjoyable day. He had lunched at the Wellands', hoping for some time alone with May. He wanted to tell her how beautiful she had looked the night before, and to beg her to bring forward the date of their marriage, which was planned for next autumn. But when he mentioned the idea at lunch, Mrs Welland had just shaken her head at him in hurt surprise, saying, 'May needs twelve sets of everything, and every piece must be sewn by hand . . .'

Then he had been forced to go with the ladies on their afternoon of social visits, calling on several families in turn to announce the engagement. As he left the Wellands' house, May's mother called after him, 'Tomorrow we'll do the Chiverses and the Dallases.' And to his horror Newland realized her plan was to visit the friends of both families in alphabetical order, and that they were only in the first quarter of the alphabet. He knew he would not enjoy the next few months.

He had meant to tell May of the Countess's request – or command, rather – that he should call on her that afternoon, but in the short time they had been alone, he had had more urgent things to say to May, and the moment for telling her had passed.

The door was opened by a dark-haired servant girl, who did not speak English. She showed him into a sitting room, and disappeared. Newland looked around curiously. The room was unlike any he had known. There were a few pieces of fine old furniture, some Italian-looking pictures, and just two roses in a tall thin vase, perfectly positioned. The room had its own special atmosphere which seemed to wrap around him – even the smell was different, suggesting exotic places like Samarkand in central Asia. 'How will May furnish our house?' he thought. 'Probably in the same purple and yellow as at her parents'. At least I'll be able to arrange my library as I like.'

After a while he heard a carriage arrive outside, and looking through the curtains he caught sight of Julius Beaufort helping Madame Olenska out. In a few moments she entered the room.

'How do you like my funny house?' she asked, showing no surprise at seeing him. 'To me it's like heaven.'

'You've arranged it delightfully,' he said.

'I suppose what I like is the wonderful feeling of being here in my own country and my own town, of being alone in it.'

'You like being alone so much?'

'Yes, as long as my friends prevent me from feeling lonely.' She sat down, lying back in her chair and putting her hands behind her head. 'This is the hour I like best, don't you?'

A sense of his own importance made him say, 'I was afraid you'd forgotten the time. Beaufort must have been a very interesting companion.'

She looked amused. 'Why – have you waited long? Mr Beaufort took me to see some houses – my family want me to move to a better area. But what does it matter where one lives?'

'This street just isn't fashionable.'

'Fashionable! Do you all think so much of that? Why not make one's own fashions? But I suppose I've lived too independently. Now I want to do what you all do. I want to feel cared for and safe.'

He was touched. 'That's what your friends want you to feel.' But he suspected she still did not realize how close to social disaster she had been, before the van der Luydens had saved her. So he said, 'Last night the best families in New York were looking after you.'

'I know, it was such a nice party!' she replied lightly.

These words were hardly adequate, Newland felt, for the social importance of that event.

'The van der Luydens,' he said seriously, 'are the most influential people in New York. Unfortunately, because they are elderly and in poor health, they do not often receive guests.'

'Isn't that the reason for their great influence?' she said thoughtfully. 'It's because they are hardly ever seen.'

He stared at her, and suddenly realized she was right. He laughed, and thought no more about the van der Luydens.

'But you'll explain these things to me, won't you?' Madame Olenska continued. 'You'll tell me all I ought to know?'

'It's you who are telling me, opening my eyes to things I've looked at so long that I no longer really see them.' He wanted to say, 'Don't be seen driving about the streets with Beaufort,' but he was being too deeply drawn into the atmosphere of the room to give advice of that kind. He felt a long way from New

York; he was in Samarkand, from where New York looked strangely small and distant, as indeed it would.

The Countess bent over the fire, holding her thin hands out to the flames, and her face seemed pale in the firelight.

'Your family,' Newland added, 'can advise you, especially the older women.'

She shook her head. 'Oh, I know! All my aunts, and my grandmother. But only if they don't hear anything unpleasant! Does no one want to know the truth here, Mr Archer? The real loneliness is living among all these kind people who only ask me to pretend!' She put her head in her hands and started crying.

'Madame Olenska! Oh, don't, Ellen!' he cried, jumping up and bending over her. He took one of her hands, holding and rubbing it like a child's, but she soon freed herself and looked up at him with wet eyes.

'Does no one cry here, either? I suppose there's no need to, in heaven,' she said with a laugh.

Newland realized with horror that he had called her 'Ellen'. The use of first names between young people was only permitted if they were engaged. Somewhere in his mind's eye he could see the tall white figure of May Welland – she seemed very far away.

Suddenly the servant came in and spoke in Italian to the Countess. She showed in a strange-looking couple – the Duke of St Austrey and Mrs Struthers, a large lady with unnaturally black hair, painted lips, and an expensive fur coat. They had come to invite Madame Olenska to a musical evening at Mrs Struthers' house on Sunday evening. Madame Olenska accepted with delight, and Mrs Struthers waved a cheerful hand at Newland.

'And bring your young gentleman with you,' she said.

Newland escaped as quickly as he could. He had no wish to

become involved with the socially unacceptable Mrs Struthers. As he went out into the wintry night, the feeling of Samarkand disappeared. New York was all around him again, and May Welland the loveliest woman in it.

He went straight to a flower shop, to send her the daily box of sweet-smelling white flowers, which he realized he had forgotten to send that morning. While in the shop, he noticed a huge bunch of yellow roses. They were not May's kind of flower – too rich, too strong, too exotic for her. He gave the assistant the Countess's address and told him to send them there at once, but he did not like to put his name on the card.

The next day he persuaded May to escape for a walk in the park. It was a sunny winter's day, with snow on the ground, and the cold air brought out the colour in May's lovely face. Newland felt proud to have such beauty walking next to him, and he felt his doubts and worries disappear.

They talked about the flowers he sent her every day, and he confessed that he had sent roses to the Countess. May was delighted he was being so kind to her cousin. Then Newland started talking about their own plans, their future, and Mrs Welland's insistence on a long engagement.

'But aren't we very happy as we are?' May asked, smiling brilliantly up at him.

'We could be even happier. We could be together all the time. We could be travelling.'

'That would be lovely,' she replied. 'But Mother would not understand us wanting to do things so differently from other couples.'

Suddenly he felt quite desperate. Would he ever be able to

reach the real May Welland, through the wall of custom and social expectation which divided them? And what if, when he finally broke down the wall, there was nobody there?

'Do we have to do things the way everyone else does?' he cried, almost wildly. 'Can't you and I be different, May?'

'But aren't we very happy as we are?' May asked.

Her eyes rested on him with a bright, unclouded admiration. 'But we can't just run away together, can we?' she asked. 'You know, like people in books.'

'Why not – why not – why not?'

She looked a little bored by his insistence. 'I'm not clever enough to argue with you. But that sort of thing is rather – vulgar, isn't it?'

'Are you so much afraid of being vulgar?'

She was clearly shocked by his question. 'Of course I am – and so are you,' she replied sharply. Then, sure of having found the right way to close the discussion, she went on light-heartedly: 'Oh, did I tell you that I showed Ellen my ring? She thinks it's the most beautiful one she ever saw . . .'

All next day he felt depressed. He could see his life stretching tidily ahead of him, with no excitement, no unplanned events, and he was filled with unreasoning horror at the thought of doing the same thing every day at the same hour. The word 'sameness!' repeated itself maddeningly inside his head.

In the afternoon Janey came to see him in his library.

'Newland, Mother's very angry,' she said.

'Angry? With whom? About what?'

'Your friend Madame Olenska. She was at Mrs Struthers' party last night, on a Sunday evening, Newland, when people are at church. She went with the Duke and Mr Julius Beaufort.'

When he heard the last name, a senseless anger took hold of Newland, but he controlled himself and just laughed. 'Well, what of it? I knew she meant to go.'

Janey went pale. 'You knew she meant to go and you didn't try to stop her? To warn her?'

'Stop her? Warn her?' He laughed again. 'I'm not engaged to the Countess Olenska!' The words sounded strange in his ears.

'Well, I think you'd better come down and speak to Mother.'

In the sitting room Mrs Archer was looking very anxious. 'I'm so worried the van der Luydens will be offended,' she said.

'Why should they be offended?' Newland asked.

'Because she went to the house of that vulgar woman.'

'Well, Mrs Struthers may be vulgar,' said Newland, 'but she has good music, and amuses people on Sunday evenings, when the whole of New York is dying of boredom.'

'Good music? All I know is, there was a woman who got up on a table and sang the things they sing at the places you go to in Paris. There was smoking and champagne.'

'Well, that kind of thing happens in other places, and the world still goes on.'

At this moment in the argument the servant came to the door and announced, 'Mr Henry van der Luyden.'

A visit from this gentleman was such an unusual event that both ladies looked quite frightened, but Newland remained calm. 'Come in, sir,' he said, going forward to greet his relation. 'We were just talking about you – and the Countess Olenska.'

Mrs Archer went pale, and put a hand to her heart.

'Ah – a delightful woman,' replied Mr van der Luyden. 'I have just been to see her. The Duke told me to go and see how cleverly she's arranged her sitting room. And it's true – quite remarkable! I would take Louisa to see the Countess if the area were less unpleasant.' There was dead silence. Mr van der Luyden continued, 'The fact is, between ourselves, I wanted to give her a friendly warning about allowing the Duke, or anyone else, to carry her off to parties with him.'

'Has the Duke been carrying her off to parties?' asked Mrs Archer innocently.

'I'm afraid so, dear Adeline. But Madame Olenska was very grateful for my few words of guidance.'

And so Mrs Archer's anxiety about Ellen Olenska's behaviour was calmed, for the moment, at least.

Two weeks later Newland was sitting doing nothing in the offices of Letterblair, Lamson and Low, the firm of lawyers whom he worked for, when he was called to the private office of the head of the firm, Mr Letterblair. The old man was clearly a little worried. It appeared that the Countess Olenska wished to get a divorce from her husband. Her family, especially old Mrs Manson Mingott, wanted to avoid the scandal this would cause. They had sent a number of papers to Mr Letterblair, asking that Newland Archer, as a future member of the family, should take on the case. They wanted Newland, on behalf of the Letterblair firm, to advise the Countess against divorce.

Newland was at first unwilling to get involved in the Countess's private life. But once he had read the papers, which included letters from her husband, he was so horrified by her suffering at the hands of the Count that he agreed to take on the case. He was determined to give her his support, no matter what she decided to do. So he made an appointment with her, at her house, in order to discuss the case.

CHAPTER 4

A SECOND VISIT TO THE COUNTESS

As Newland walked up Fifth Avenue after dinner that evening, he could see a number of carriages outside the Chiverses', where they were having a party for the Duke. He passed the Beauforts' house, and saw Julius himself come out and drive away in his carriage.

'Probably on his way to that new lady friend of his,' thought Newland. All of New York knew about Beaufort's mistresses, and Miss Fanny Ring was the latest in a long line.

He walked on into the narrow street where the Countess lived, surrounded by the houses of painters and writers. He and his family belonged to the part of New York society that believed in the importance of literature and art, but fashionable and well-born families rarely mixed socially with artists. Newland himself knew many artists and musicians, whom he met in the little bars and clubs which were beginning to open in the back streets, but he would never expect to meet them in a gentleman's house. He imagined that the Countess, whose house was full of books, was used to a much more open society, where writers and artists came and went freely, and that this might be one of the things she would miss from her old life.

He reached her house and was let in by the servant girl, who was smiling mysteriously. In the hall was a fur-lined coat and a silk opera-hat with the letters J.B. in gold on it; it was clear that Julius Beaufort was visiting Madame Olenska. Newland was so angry that he almost left at once. But then he remembered he had not told the Countess he wished to see her privately, so he could not blame her for opening her doors to other visitors.

In the sitting room Beaufort was standing in front of the fire, smiling down at the Countess. She was half lying on a sofa, her head supported on one hand; her sleeve had fallen away to leave her white arm visible up to the elbow. Instead of the usual close-fitting, all-covering silk dress which New York ladies wore when receiving evening visitors, she was wearing a long dress of soft red material, with black fur around the neck and down the front. The effect was certainly pleasing.

'Well, well – three whole days at Skuytercliff!' Beaufort was saying in his loud voice as Newland entered. Skuytercliff was the van der Luydens' country house, just outside New York, and it seemed the Countess was invited there. 'It's a pity – you'll miss the musical evening I've planned for you on Sunday.'

She held out her hand to greet Newland, as she replied to Beaufort. 'Ah, that does tempt me! Except for the other evening at Mrs Struthers', I've not met a single artist since I've been here.'

'I know one or two painters, very nice people, who I could bring to see you if you'd allow me,' said Newland daringly.

'Painters in New York?' asked Beaufort with a laugh. He gave the impression there were none, since he did not buy their pictures. And Madame Olenska said to Newland, 'That would be delightful. But I was thinking of singers, actors, musicians. My husband's house was always full of them.'

Newland felt confused – how could she speak so calmly of her married life? But he was pleased to see she wanted to speak to him privately, because she made it clear to Beaufort that he must leave. And a few minutes later they were alone together.

'So you care for painting, then?' she began by asking.

'Oh yes, enormously. When I'm in Paris or London, I never miss a show. I try to see all the new pictures.'

'My life used to be full of such things too. But now I want to throw off my old life, to become just like everybody else here.'

Newland reddened. 'You'll never be like everybody else.'

'Ah, don't say that! If you knew how I hate to be different!' Her face looked dark and sad as she spoke.

He waited a moment and cleared his throat. 'I know you want – a divorce. Mr Letterblair told me. That's why I've come. You see, I'm in the firm.'

Her eyes brightened. 'You mean you can manage it for me? I can talk to you instead of to Mr Letterblair? Oh, that will be so much easier! You'll help me, won't you?'

'First . . .' he hesitated, 'perhaps I ought to know a little more.'

She seemed surprised. 'You've read the papers? You know about my husband's mistresses? What could be worse than that? Our church allows divorce in such cases.'

'That's true, but . . .' Newland was thinking of a letter from the Count he had read, accusing his wife of having had an affair with his secretary. How much truth was there in that? Only Ellen could tell. 'Of course, you know that if your husband chooses to fight the case, as he threatens to, he can say things . . .'

'Yes?'

'Things that . . . that might be – disagreeable – to you, and say them publicly – even if they aren't true.'

'What harm could such accusations, even if he made them publicly, do me here in New York?'

Newland thought, 'She still knows so little about us!' He tried to explain. 'This is a very small world, compared to the one you've lived in. Our ideas about marriage and divorce are particularly old-fashioned, especially if the woman has . . . put herself, by some unusual behaviour, in a position where – where offensive accusations can be made against her.'

Her head bent down low, and Newland waited, hoping desperately for a little anger, or at least just a word to tell him that no accusation would be true. No word came.

A clock ticked softly in a corner, and the whole room seemed to be waiting silently with Newland.

'Yes,' she whispered at last. 'That's what my family say. And you're one of them, or will be soon. Do you share their view?'

He looked away from her for a moment. How could he say, 'Yes, if what your husband says is true'?

Instead he said gently, 'Is a divorce really worth it, when there's the possibility – the certainty – of a lot of unpleasantness?'

'But my freedom – isn't that worth it?'

'It's my business, you know, to help you to see these things as the people who are fondest of you see them.' He was filling the silence with meaningless talk. He could do nothing else, since she would not or could not say the one word that would have cleared the air, and told him the truth.

Suddenly she stood up. 'Very well, I will do what you wish,' she said.

The blood rushed to his face, and he caught her hands in his. 'I . . . I do want to help you,' he said.

'You do help me. Good night, my cousin.'

He bent and kissed her hands, which were cold and lifeless. When she took them away, he turned to the door, found his coat and hat in the hall, and ran out into the winter night, bursting with unspoken words.

A week later Newland was at Wallack's theatre, watching one of that season's most popular plays. He had seen it several times, and one particular scene was his favourite. He was watching it now. In a room, two lovers said goodbye, sadly, almost wordlessly, and the man started towards the door. The woman turned away from him to the fireplace and looked down into the fire. She was wearing a long grey dress with long black ribbons falling down her back. At the door her lover turned for one last look at her; then he walked quietly back, lifted one of the ribbons, kissed it, and left the room without her hearing him or changing her position. And on this silent parting the curtain fell.

Newland thought this as fine as anything he had ever seen in the theatres of Paris and London. The silence and the dumb misery of the lovers' goodbye moved him greatly. And it reminded him – he could not have said why – of his goodbye to Madame Olenska after their conversation a week earlier.

When he had left her, he had the feeling that Count Olenski's accusation was almost certainly true. Ellen was young, she was frightened, she was desperate – what more natural than that she should be grateful to her rescuer? The pity was that, in the law's eyes and the world's, one affair with the secretary made her as wicked as her husband, with his many mistresses. And Newland had explained to her that simple, kind-hearted New York was exactly the place where she could least hope for understanding.

Having to make these facts plain to her, and watching her miserable acceptance of them, had been extremely painful to him. He was glad that he alone knew her secret, which would have horribly embarrassed her relations. And when he told her family she had decided not to ask for a divorce, they were all very grateful to him for sparing them so much unpleasantness.

These thoughts reminded him so strongly of his last talk with Madame Olenska that, as the curtain fell on the lovers' parting, his eyes filled with tears and he stood up to leave the theatre. In doing so, he saw Madame Olenska in a box with the Beauforts and some other people. He had tried to avoid meeting her socially, but now their eyes met, and as Mrs Beaufort waved to him to join them, it was impossible to refuse.

He greeted the Beauforts, but soon found himself sitting beside the Countess. She turned and spoke to him in a low voice.

'Do you think,' she asked, looking towards the stage, 'the lover will send her a bunch of yellow roses tomorrow morning?'

Newland reddened and his heart jumped in surprise. He had visited her only twice and each time had sent her yellow roses, but without giving his name. She had never mentioned them before. Now the fact that she knew he had sent them, and connected them to the scene they had just watched, filled him with pleasure.

'I was thinking of that too,' he said.

To his surprise she blushed, and said after a pause, 'What do you do when May is away?'

'I get on with my work,' he replied, a little annoyed by the question. The Wellands always spent February in Florida, as their doctor considered the warm weather there necessary for Mr Welland's chest, and they were there now. Newland had realized there was no chance of persuading them to break the habit of a lifetime, so he had not tried. He would have liked to go with them, but he too was tied by custom and habit – no serious-minded young men took holidays in mid-winter.

He was conscious Madame Olenska was looking at him. 'I understand – that you were right about the divorce,' she said a little breathlessly. 'But sometimes – life is difficult.'

'I know.'

'And I wanted to tell you that I do feel you were right, and that I'm grateful to you.' She lifted her opera-glasses quickly to her eyes as she heard Beaufort coming to sit next to her.

Newland stood up, and left the box and the theatre.

The day before, he had received a letter from May, in which she had asked him to be kind to Ellen in her absence. 'She likes and admires you so much, and although she doesn't show it, she's very lonely and unhappy. You're almost the only person in New York who can talk to her about what she really cares for.'

His wise May – how he loved her for that letter! But he did not want, as an engaged man, to be too obviously the Countess's defender and companion. She could probably take care of herself better than May imagined – she had several gentlemen around her who would be only too glad to be of assistance. But even so, he never saw her without feeling that, after all, May was right. Ellen Olenska was lonely and she was unhappy.

The next morning Newland searched the flower shops for yellow roses, but found none. As a result of this search, he arrived late at the office, and noticed that his lateness made no difference at all to anyone. He was filled with sudden despair at the uselessness of his life. He was just one of the many young men in the old-fashioned law firms like Mr Letterblair's, who sat at their desks or simply read the newspapers for a certain number of hours every day. They didn't need to earn money, but it was thought that young men should have something to do, and the law, being a profession, was considered to be more suitable work for a gentleman than business. Few of them had any ambition, and over many of them the grey dullness of an empty life was already spreading.

It made Newland cold with fear to think it might be spreading over him too. 'I'll never do anything worthwhile!' he thought angrily. 'And my interest in books and paintings and music, my European travels – will I be able to keep any of that up when I'm married?' He thought about men he knew – men who in their younger days had been full of hopes and dreams, as he was now. 'And what happened to them?' he thought. 'Their lives became nothing more than one long, mindless, comfortable routine of dinners and visits and evening parties.'

From his office he sent a note to Madame Olenska, asking if he could call on her that afternoon, but he received no reply that day or the next. This unexpected silence made him unreasonably angry. On the third morning he received a note from her, and to his surprise it had been posted from Skuytercliff. It said:

I ran away the day after I saw you at the theatre, and these
kind friends are allowing me to stay here as long as I like. I
wanted to be quiet, and think things over. I feel so safe here.
I wish you were with us. Yours sincerely, Ellen Olenska

'What is she running away from?' he wondered. 'And why does she feel the need to be safe? However, she's certainly made an impression on the van der Luydens – they don't usually encourage their visitors to stay longer than a weekend.'

He felt disappointed that she was away. Then he remembered that he had an invitation from the Chiverses to spend this weekend with them at their country house, Highbank, which was not far from Skuytercliff. He wrote a hurried telegram and sent it off at once, accepting the invitation.

CHAPTER 5
MAY SURPRISES NEWLAND

At Highbank Newland was a dutiful guest until lunch on Sunday, when he borrowed a carriage and drove over to Skuytercliff.

The van der Luydens' large country house never looked particularly welcoming, and now in the depths of winter it looked even less so. The servant who opened the door explained that Mrs van der Luyden and the Countess were at church. Newland said he would walk to the church to meet the ladies.

And as he walked along the path, he was delighted to see a figure in a red coat coming towards him. He hurried forward, and Madame Olenska stopped short with a smile of welcome.

'Ah, you've come!' she said, giving him her hand. 'Mrs van der Luyden has gone on to visit some friends, so I'm alone.'

The red coat made her look brilliantly pretty, like the Ellen of the old days. He replied, 'I came to see what you were running away from.'

Her smile disappeared, but she answered, 'You'll see soon.' She added, more cheerfully, 'What does it matter, now that you're here to protect me?'

The blood rose to his face and he caught the sleeve of her coat. 'Ellen, what is it? You must tell me.'

'Oh, let's run a race first! My feet are freezing!' And she ran away from him, her red coat bright against the snow. Newland started after her, and they met, laughing, under a tree.

38

She looked up at him and smiled. 'I knew you'd come.'

'That shows you wanted me to,' he replied, his heart beating wildly with delight.

They walked along together. The ground seemed to sing under their feet, and there was a mysterious brightness in the air.

'May asked you to take care of me,' she said after a while.

Ellen looked up at Newland and smiled. 'I knew you'd come.'

'I didn't need any asking.'

'Ah – what a poor, helpless, defenceless thing you must all think I am! But women here seem not to feel the need.'

He lowered his voice to ask, 'What sort of need?'

'Ah, don't ask me! I don't speak your language.'

He stood still on the path, looking down at her. 'What did I come for, if I don't speak yours?'

'Oh, my friend . . . !' She laid her hand lightly on his arm.

'Ellen, why won't you tell me what's happened?'

'I will tell you, but where? One can't be alone for a minute in that enormous house, with servants always in and out of every room! Is there nowhere in an American house where one may be by oneself? You're all so shy and yet so public at the same time.'

'Ah, you don't like us!' said Newland sadly.

Just then they passed an ancient stone house, called the Patroon's house, which the first owner of Skuytercliff had built and lived in, three hundred years before. The van der Luydens kept it to show to their visitors as a place of historical interest.

'What luck!' cried Ellen. 'We can go in and have a quiet talk. Someone's even lit a fire. No one will disturb us there.'

They went in and sat down by a bright fire.

'When you wrote to me, you were unhappy,' said Newland, watching her expressive face.

'Yes, I was. But I can't feel unhappy when you're here.'

'I shan't be here very long.' His lips felt stiff with the effort of saying just so much and no more.

'I know. But I live in the moment when I'm happy. I don't look ahead.'

The words stole through him like a temptation. He got up and stood looking out through the window, with his back to her.

What if she had been running away from *him*, and she had waited to tell him until they were alone together in this secret place?

'Ellen, please tell me. Tell me who you're running away from.'

For a long moment she was silent, and in that moment Newland imagined her, almost heard her, stealing up behind him to throw her light arms around his neck. But while he waited, his whole mind and body ready for that wonderful thing to happen, he saw a heavily-coated man walking along the path to the house. The man was Julius Beaufort.

'Ah!' said Newland, bursting into a laugh. 'So that's it?'

Madame Olenska ran to his side, slipping her hand into his, but when she saw Beaufort, her face went pale. 'I didn't know he was here,' she whispered. Her hand still held Newland's, but he drew away from her and, walking into the hall, threw open the door of the little house. 'Come in, Beaufort, this way! Madame Olenska is expecting you!' he said.

During his journey back to New York the next day, Newland thought bitterly of Beaufort. He was clearly the man Ellen was running away from. He was chasing her, and Julius Beaufort only ever had one purpose in mind when chasing pretty women.

The next two or three days went by very slowly. There were moments when Newland felt he was being buried alive under his future. He heard nothing from Ellen until the fourth evening, when a note from her arrived at his house. It said simply:

Come late tomorrow. I must explain to you. Ellen

The young man spent all night thinking about the note. There were several ways of answering it. The reply he finally decided on, at sunrise, was to pack a bag with some clothes and jump on a boat which was leaving that day for Florida.

When he walked down the sandy main street of St Augustine and saw May Welland standing there with the sun in her hair, he wondered why he had waited so long to come. Here was truth, here was reality, here was the life that belonged to him!

'Newland – has anything happened?' she asked.

'Yes – I found I had to see you,' he replied, and she blushed happily. They sat down on a bench under some orange trees, and he put his arm round her waist and kissed her. It was like drinking from a cool mountain stream on a hot summer's day.

He explained to May's parents that he had come because he felt he might be getting a cold. Mr Welland understood all anxiety over health only too well, and insisted he should stay at least a week with them, to prevent any possible illness taking hold.

He walked and read and went boating with May in the warm Florida sunshine. All the time he was thinking about their wedding, which seemed unimaginably far away.

The day before he left, they were walking through the orange trees again, when suddenly he burst out, 'Can't you understand, May? I want to make our dreams real! I want you to be my wife, now rather than later, this year rather than next!'

For a moment May was silent. Then, clear-eyed, she looked straight at him. 'I'm not sure I *do* understand. Is it – is it because you're not certain of continuing to care for me?'

Newland was shocked into saying, 'My God – perhaps – I don't know!' Both were silent for a moment.

'If that is it – then, is there someone else? Let us talk honestly, Newland. I've felt a difference in you since our engagement was announced.'

'My dear, what madness!' he managed to say.

'It won't hurt us to talk about it. You could so easily have made a mistake – anyone can.'

'If I had made a mistake of the kind you suggest, is it likely I would be begging you to marry me sooner?'

She thought for a moment. 'Yes,' she said at last. 'You might want to decide the matter, once and for all.'

Her calm intelligence took his breath away, but he could see how painful this was for her. She continued, 'You know, a girl sees more than her parents imagine. I've always known there was someone in your past. I saw her once – her face was sad and I felt sorry for her – and I remembered that when we got engaged.'

'My dear child – is that all? If you only knew the truth!'

'Then there is a truth I don't know?'

'I mean, the truth about that old story.'

'But that's what I want to know. Newland, I couldn't build my happiness on a wrong done to another woman! I understand that when two people really love each other, they might have to go against public opinion. And if you feel yourself in any way – promised to that woman – and if there is any way you can keep your word – even by her getting a divorce, then, Newland, don't give her up because of me!'

He had never admired May so much as at that moment. How brave of her to speak so plainly, and how generous to offer to give him up to his former mistress! But with all her intelligence, she had not seen what was troubling him.

'There was no promise of the kind you think. But I love you for saying that. I mean, every woman's right to her freedom—'
He stopped, surprised by the direction his thoughts were taking.

May turned her blushing face towards him, and as he bent to kiss her, he saw her eyes were full of happy tears. For a moment he had seen a woman who could think for herself, a woman who was prepared to break away from society's rules. But the next moment he was disappointed to see the old, dutiful May return. She seemed to be aware of his disappointment, but without knowing what to do about it. They walked silently home.

Two days after his return to New York, Newland called on old Mrs Manson Mingott, to persuade her to use her influence with the Wellands about an early wedding date for him and May. She was amused by his urgency, and agreed to help. The Countess, who was visiting her grandmother, was also there, and listened thoughtfully to this conversation. Newland had a few minutes alone with her, when she walked with him to the front door.

'When can I see you?' he asked in a low voice.

'Whenever you like, but it must be soon if you want to see the little house again. I'm moving next week.'

For a moment he was back again in the exotic atmosphere of her sitting room. 'Tomorrow evening?' he asked.

'Tomorrow, yes, but come early. I'm going out later.'

It was only half-past eight when he arrived at her house. In the sitting room he found Medora Manson, Ellen's aunt, who had just arrived back from a long trip to Cuba. She greeted him, and while they waited for Ellen to join them, told him she had a letter from the Count to give to her niece. 'Yes, my poor, foolish Olenski,' she added, 'all he asks is to take her back as his wife!'

'Good God!' cried Newland, jumping up.

'You are horrified? Of course I do not defend him. But just think what she is giving up if she stays here! Palaces, jewels, art, priceless furniture, music, brilliant conversation – forgive me, my dear young man, but one does not find that here. The truth is, Mr Archer, I have heard of your influence over dear Ellen, and I hoped I might count on your support – to persuade you . . .'

'That she ought to go back? I would rather see her dead!' cried the young man violently.

'Ah,' said Mrs Manson calmly. 'Am I to understand you prefer *that*?' She pointed to a huge bunch of expensive flowers on the sofa, with Beaufort's card just visible. 'After all, marriage is marriage . . . and my niece is still a wife . . .'

At that moment Ellen appeared in the doorway.

'We were saying, my dear,' smiled Mrs Manson, 'here is something a fond admirer has sent you.'

Madame Olenska turned, saw the flowers, and a silent anger seemed to run through her. She rang for her servant and told her to take them to a neighbour who was ill. 'Take them at once!' she cried. 'I don't want them in the house!' She turned to Newland. 'Mr Archer, my aunt is just leaving. Would you take her to the carriage? I'll leave myself when the carriage comes back.'

When he returned, the Countess was sitting by the fire.

'Your aunt thinks you will go back to your husband,' he said.

'Many cruel things have been believed of me.'

'Oh Ellen – forgive me – I'm a fool!'

'I know you have your own troubles. You think the Wellands are unreasonable about your marriage, and of course I agree with you.' He realized she was changing the subject.

'Yes. I went south to ask May to shorten the engagement. We had an honest talk, our first, in fact. She thinks my impatience is a bad sign. She thinks it means I want to marry her at once to get away from someone whom I – care for more.'

'But if she thinks that, why isn't she in a hurry too?'

'Because she's not like that. She's so much nobler. She has offered to give me up, for the other woman.'

Madame Olenska looked into the fire for some time. Down the quiet street Newland could hear her horses returning.

'That *is* noble,' she said.

'Yes. But I don't intend to marry anyone else.'

'Ah.' There was another long pause. 'This other woman – does she love you?'

'Oh, there's no other woman. I mean, the person May was thinking of was never—'

'Then why, after all, are you in such a hurry to marry?'

'There's your carriage,' said Newland.

'Yes, I should go. I am expected at Mrs Struthers'. I must go where I am invited, or I shall be too lonely.' She smiled a little.

Newland did not want her to leave. 'May guessed the truth,' he said. 'There *is* another woman – but not the one she thinks.'

She did not answer, and did not move. He sat down beside her and took her hand. But she jumped up and freed her hand.

'Don't make love to me! Too many men have done that!'

It was the bitterest thing she could have said to him.

'I have never made love to you, and I never shall. But you are the woman I would have married if it had been possible.'

'But it's you who've made it impossible!' she cried.

He stared at her, his mind full of darkness in which there was a single point of blinding light.

'*I've* made it impossible?'

'You, you, *you*!' Her lips were trembling. 'You made me give up the idea of divorce, to spare my family the publicity, the scandal. And because my family was going to become your family, I did what you told me. I did it for you, and for May!'

'Good God!' he cried. 'And I thought . . . oh, don't ask me what I thought!'

She blushed deeply. 'But I do ask you.'

'There were accusations in your husband's letter . . .'

'I had nothing to fear from that letter, absolutely nothing! All I feared was to bring scandal on the family, on you and May.'

'Good God!' he cried again, putting his face in his hands.

The silence that followed lay on them like a gravestone, and it seemed to Newland that nothing would ever lift that load from

'You are the woman I would have married if it had been possible,'
said Newland.

47

his heart. He did not move, or raise his head from his hands.

'At least I loved you!' he said, out of the darkness.

On the other side of the room, he heard a sound like a child crying softly. He ran to her.

'Ellen! What madness is this? Why are you crying? Nothing's done that can't be undone. I'm still free, and you're going to be.' He had her in his arms, her face like a wet flower at his lips. Why, oh why, had he stood for five minutes arguing with her across the room, when just touching her made everything so simple?

She gave him back all his kiss, but after a moment he felt her stiffening in his arms, and she put him aside.

'Ah, my poor Newland – I suppose this had to happen. But it doesn't change things in the least.'

'It changes the whole of life for me.'

'No, it mustn't, it can't. You're engaged to May Welland, and I'm married to the Count.'

Newland stood up. 'Nonsense! It's too late for that sort of thing. We've no right to lie to other people or ourselves.'

'You say that because it's the easiest thing to say at the moment. In reality it's too late to do anything but what we'd both decided on. You see, from the very beginning I realized how kind, how noble you were. Very good people don't impress me – I feel they've never been tempted. But *you* know, you understand, you've felt the world outside, tempting you with its golden hands – and yet you won't accept happiness bought with cruelty. That's better, nobler, than anything I've ever known.'

She spoke quietly, without tears, and each word burnt its way into Newland's heart. 'Don't let us undo what you've done!' she cried. 'I can't go back now to that other way of thinking. I can't love you unless I give you up.'

They remained, facing each other, divided by the distance her words had created. Suddenly, he was angry. 'And Beaufort? Is he to replace me? You're seeing him this evening, aren't you?'

'I shall not go out this evening,' she said calmly.

'You tell me you're lonely – I've no right to keep you from your friends,' he said bitterly.

'I shan't be lonely now. I *was* lonely, I *was* afraid. But the emptiness and darkness are gone now.'

He turned away, with a sense of complete exhaustion.

At that moment the doorbell rang, and a minute later the servant came in with a telegram for the Countess. It said:

GRANDMOTHER'S TELEGRAM SUCCESSFUL. PARENTS AGREE WEDDING AFTER EASTER. TOO HAPPY FOR WORDS AND LOVE YOU DEARLY. YOUR GRATEFUL MAY

Half an hour later, when Newland unlocked his own front door, he found a similar telegram waiting for him in the hall, saying:

PARENTS AGREE WEDDING TUESDAY AFTER EASTER GRACE CHURCH. SO HAPPY. LOVE MAY

He started laughing wildly and could not stop. He was making so much noise that his sister came out of her bedroom.

'Newland, whatever is the matter? It's very late!'

'Nothing's the matter, Janey, except that I'm going to be married in a month!'

Janey fell on his neck and pressed him to her thin chest. 'Oh, Newland, how wonderful! I'm so glad! But why do you keep on laughing? Do stop, or you'll wake Mother.'

CHAPTER 6
THE WEDDING AND BEYOND

The sun shone weakly down on Grace Church, and a light spring wind blew dust everywhere. Inside the church almost every seat was taken, and in the centre stood the bridegroom and his best man, waiting for the bride to arrive.

Newland was familiar with the preparations necessary for a fashionable New York wedding, as he had often been a best man himself at his friends' weddings. For his own wedding he had obeyed all his best man's commands, following his instructions down to the last detail. It was easier to obey blindly than to think, to doubt, to question. 'I've sent flowers to the eight bridesmaids,' he thought, 'I've written thank-you letters for the wedding presents, paid for the use of the church, and made arrangements for the honeymoon. I think I've done everything.'

'Got the ring all right?' whispered his best man, looking pale. He was feeling the heaviness of the responsibility.

Newland did what he had seen so many bridegrooms do – feel quickly in a jacket pocket – and found the little gold ring, which had *Newland to May, April 22, 1874* written inside.

He looked at the faces he knew so well in the seats all around him. 'How like a first night at the opera,' he thought, 'waiting for the curtain to rise!' He saw his mother and Janey, crying with happiness, he saw Julius Beaufort next to his beautiful wife, he saw Lawrence Lefferts, the expert on 'form'. He wondered how many social mistakes Lefferts' eager eyes would discover during

50

the wedding, and then he suddenly remembered that he too had once thought such things important. A stormy discussion about whether the wedding presents should be put on show to the guests had darkened the last hours before the wedding, and it seemed unbelievable to him that adults could get so angry over something so meaningless. Yet there was a time when he had had just as strongly-felt opinions on such matters.

'And all the while, I suppose,' he thought, 'real people were living somewhere, and real things were happening to them . . .'

'*She's coming!*' the best man whispered excitedly, but Newland knew better. It was true the great doors had opened, but only for the arrival of May's family, not the bride herself.

As the family came in, there was a thin older woman, who almost made his heart stop beating. Medora Manson and her niece were now living in Washington, and neither of them was expected at the wedding. Newland stared hard at Medora, trying to see who came behind her. There was no one.

'Newland – I say – *she's here!*' said the best man.

Newland realized he had been in a kind of dream for the last few minutes, because the bride, on her father's arm, with her bridesmaids behind her, was already halfway towards him. He opened his eyes and felt his heart begin to beat normally again. The music, the flowers, the cloud-like figure all in white coming closer, all these sights and sounds, so familiar in themselves, so very strange to him today, were making him feel confused.

'My God,' he thought, '*have* I got the ring?' and once more he did what all bridegrooms do, desperately pushing his hand down into his pocket until his fingers touched gold.

Then, in a moment, May was beside him, looking so beautiful that he stood a little straighter and smiled into her eyes.

A short time later, the ring was on her finger, and they were ready to walk through the church past their smiling friends and then out into the sunshine as man and wife. 'Your arm – *give her your arm*!' whispered the best man, and once more Newland

The bride, on her father's arm, was already halfway towards him.

came back to reality. 'What was it that set me dreaming this time?' he wondered. Perhaps it was seeing a dark-haired lady at the back of the church, who, when she turned round, was laughably unlike the person he was thinking of.

And now he and his wife were getting into the carriage. She turned to him with a brilliant smile and they held hands.

'Dearest!' said Newland – and suddenly a black hole opened up in front of him and he felt himself falling deeper and deeper into it, while his voice went on speaking smoothly and cheerfully. 'Yes, I thought I'd lost the ring – well, every bridegroom thinks that, I suppose. But you *did* keep me waiting, you know. I had time to think of every horror that might possibly happen.'

She surprised him by throwing her arms round his neck, right in the middle of Fifth Avenue. 'But none *can* ever happen now, can it, Newland, as long as we two are together?'

Newland's aunts, the du Lacs, had offered the young couple their country home near Skuytercliff for the first week of the honeymoon, but when Newland and May got out of the train at the nearest station, they discovered one of the van der Luydens' servants waiting for them.

'I'm sorry, sir,' he said, 'but there's a problem with the water at the du Lacs', so Mr van der Luyden has arranged for you to stay at the Patroon's house at Skuytercliff instead.'

Newland stared at the man, unable to speak, but May's eager voice broke out, covering the embarrassed silence, 'Oh, the Patroon's house will be perfect – won't it, Newland? It's so kind of the van der Luydens to think of it!'

And as they stepped into the van der Luydens' carriage, she said to Newland, 'I've never been inside it – have you? The van der Luydens opened it to show Ellen, it seems, when she was staying at Skuytercliff. She told me it's the only house she's seen in America where she could imagine being completely happy.'

'Well, that's what we're going to be, isn't it?' cried her husband, smiling brightly.

'Ah, it's just our luck beginning,' she replied, 'the wonderful luck we're always going to have together!'

After their stay at the Patroon's house, they sailed to Europe to continue their honeymoon. They spent June in Paris, so that May could order new clothes, July in the Swiss mountains, and August in a quiet little town on the northern French coast. Their final two weeks were in London, so that Newland could order *his* clothes. They did not go to the Italian Lakes – thinking about it, Newland could not imagine his bride there. In fact, travelling interested her even less than he had expected.

Newland had decided to behave to May exactly as all his friends behaved to their wives, and to put away his thoughts about freedom for women. There was no use giving freedom to a wife who had not the smallest idea that she was *not* free. He knew that the fineness of May's feeling for him, and her nobility of character, made her a wife of whom he could be proud, but her insistence on obeying the rules of society worried him.

In London, at a dinner party given by some friends of Mrs Archer's, the Carfrys, they met a young Frenchman called Monsieur Rivière. Newland liked him, in spite of his thin, ugly face, and had an interesting conversation about books with him. Later, Newland suggested to May that they could invite the Frenchman to dinner, to continue the conversation.

May was surprised. 'But he's almost like the Carfrys' servant!

They pay him to teach French to their nephew! Why would we invite *him* to dinner? Surely not, Newland!'

Newland did not protest, because he did not feel strongly enough about it. He realized, with a sudden cold feeling inside him, that in future many problems would be solved for him in this way, and he tried to find comfort in the old saying that the first six months of marriage were always the most difficult.

When they returned from their honeymoon, and moved into the well-built, expensively furnished house Mr Welland had bought for them, life became easier for Newland. He had his routine of going to the office, and then seeing some of his friends in a bar or a club, and occasionally taking May to the theatre or the opera.

But in the spring of the following year May persuaded him that they should spend August with her parents in their comfortable beach house in fashionable Newport. Newland had agreed, because he could think of no good reason for refusing, but he knew he would not enjoy it. May reminded him that when he was single, he had enjoyed spending the summer there, and he knew it was true. He was surprised to find how much his opinions had changed since then.

But he could not say that he had been mistaken in his choice of bride. May was one of the handsomest and most popular young married women in New York, and a thoughtful, sweet-tempered companion. He had trained himself to think of his feelings for her cousin as a momentary madness, as the last of a young man's attempts to find love. It now seemed unthinkable that he could have dreamed of marrying Ellen Olenska, and she remained in his memory as the saddest of a long line of ghosts.

One day, while they were in Newport, he and May visited old Mrs Manson Mingott, who had her own house there. Newland discovered from the two women's conversation that Ellen and her aunt were spending the summer with some people called the Blenkers, at Portsmouth, a much less fashionable town further north. Then old Mrs Mingott added, 'But dear Ellen's come to spend the day with me today,' and Newland's heart almost stopped beating, as it had done at his wedding.

'She's just outside, I think,' Mrs Mingott said, and she called out through the window across the garden, 'Ellen! *Ellen*!'

There was no answer, so Mrs Mingott rang for a servant.

'Where's the Countess Olenska?' she demanded.

'Walking down to the beach, madam,' replied the servant.

The old lady turned to Newland. 'Be a good boy – run and fetch her for me,' she said. He stood up in a kind of dream – he was seeing the little fire-lit sitting room again, and hearing the sound of Ellen's horses returning down the deserted street.

He walked down to the beach, and stopped before he reached the sand. There, in front of him, on a long grassy piece of land, was a wooden summerhouse, with windows and doors open to the warm summer air. Inside the summerhouse stood a lady, looking out to sea. 'Have I just woken up?' wondered Newland. That figure from the past was a dream, and the reality was what was waiting for him away from the beach – his young wife, dinner with the Wellands, summer with the Wellands . . . 'What am I? Just a son-in-law and a husband,' he thought.

The figure in the summerhouse had not moved. For a long moment the young man stood there, watching the sailing boats out at sea. The lady seemed to be held by the same sight.

'She doesn't know – she hasn't guessed,' he thought. 'Would

I know if she came up behind me, I wonder?' And suddenly he told himself, 'If she doesn't turn before the red sail crosses in front of that rock, I'll go back up to the house.'

The boat with the red sail was moving out to sea with the tide. It moved slowly towards the rock, and then passed it. Newland waited until the sail was a long way past the rock, but still the figure in the summerhouse did not move.

He turned and walked up the hill to the house.

As they drove home in the gathering darkness, May said, 'I'm sorry you didn't find Ellen. I'd have liked to see her again. But perhaps she no longer cares for her friends. I mean, why give up New York and go to Washington? I wonder if she would be happier with her husband, after all.'

Newland burst into an angry laugh. 'That's cruel of you – you know she would suffer terribly if she went back to him!'

'It's a pity she ever married a foreigner, then,' said May calmly, sounding very like her mother. Newland did not reply.

That evening, at May's parents' home, he felt it was the Welland house, and the life he was expected to live in it, that had become unreal, while the short scene at the beach was as close to him as the blood in his body.

All that night he lay awake at May's side, watching the moonlight on the carpet, and thinking of Ellen Olenska.

CHAPTER 7

NEWLAND IN BOSTON

The next day Newland told May he was going to see about buying a new horse for her carriage, and drove north to Portsmouth. He found the Blenkers' house, but Ellen was not there. The Blenkers told him she had received a telegram the day before, and gone to Boston, where she would be staying at the Parker House Hotel.

When he returned to Newport, he told May he had urgent business in Boston. He was ashamed of the way he was able to lie so easily, but it had to be done. He travelled all night, by boat and train, and arrived in a hot and dirty midsummer Boston.

After having breakfast at a hotel, he sent a messenger to the Parker House Hotel with a note for Countess Olenska. The man returned after ten minutes. 'The lady was out, sir,' he said.

'It must be a mistake!' thought Newland. 'How could she be out so early? How stupid of me not to send a note earlier!'

He went out, and as he started to walk across the park towards Ellen's hotel, he saw her, sitting on a bench under a tree. Her head was bent low, and she looked quite miserable. He came a step nearer, and she turned and saw him.

'Oh!' she said, her face breaking into a slow smile of wonder and happiness, and she made room for him on the bench.

'I'm here on business – just got here,' Newland explained. 'But what on earth are *you* doing here?' He had really no idea what he was saying; he seemed to be shouting to her across endless distances; he thought she might disappear again before he could reach her.

'I'm here on business too,' she answered.

'You do your hair differently now,' he said, his heart beating wildly as he looked at her.

'Differently? No, it's the best I can do without my servant.'

'You didn't bring her? You're staying alone at the hotel?'

She looked at him, with a little challenging smile in her eyes. 'Does that seem so dangerous to you?'

'No, not dangerous, but—'

'But unusual? I see, I suppose it is. I hadn't thought of it, because I've just done something so much more unusual.' Her eyes still watched him with a little challenge. 'I've just refused to take back some money – which belonged to me.'

Newland jumped up and moved a step or two away. Then he came back and stood in front of her.

'Someone – has come here to meet you – with this offer?'

'Yes.'

'And you refused, because of the conditions?'

'I refused,' she said after a moment.

He sat down by her again. 'What were the conditions?'

'Oh, they were not demanding. Just to sit at the head of his dinner table now and then.'

There was another silence. Newland was searching for the right words. 'He wants you back – at any price.'

'A considerable price. At least, it's considerable for me.'

'You came to Boston in order to meet him?'

She stared, and then laughed. 'Meet him – my husband? *Here?* He spends his summers in more fashionable places.'

'He sent someone to you, with a letter?'

'Not a letter, just a message. He hardly ever writes to me.'

Newland blushed, thinking of the accusation in the only letter he knew the Count had written to her. 'Why is that?'

'Why should he write? What are secretaries for?'

The young man's blush deepened, and he was about to ask, 'Did he send his secretary, the one you ran away with?' But he stopped, in order to spare Ellen the embarrassment of replying.

'The messenger has insisted on waiting until this evening,' added Madame Olenska, smiling, 'in case I change my mind.'

'And you came out here to think things over?'

'I came out for a breath of air. The hotel's too hot. I'm taking the afternoon train back to Portsmouth.'

They sat silent, not looking at each other. Finally she turned her eyes again to his face and said, 'You've not changed.'

He felt like saying, 'I had, until I saw you again,' but instead he stood up suddenly and looked round at the untidy park.

'This is horrible. Why don't we go out in a boat? It will be cooler on the water. We could take the boat to Point Arley and back.' She looked up at him hesitatingly and he went on, 'There won't be many people on the boat. My train for New York doesn't leave until the evening. Why shouldn't we?' Suddenly he broke out, 'Haven't we done all we can?'

'Oh!' she whispered. 'You mustn't say things like that to me.'

'I'll say anything you like; or nothing. What harm can it do to anybody? All I want is to listen to you.'

She took a little gold watch from her pocket.

'Oh, don't think about time!' he cried. 'Give me the day! Come now, at once! It's a hundred years since we last met – it may be another hundred before we meet again.'

Her anxious eyes were on his face. 'Why didn't you come

down to the beach to fetch me, the day I was at Grandmother's?'

'Because you didn't look round. I wanted you to look round.' He laughed at the childishness of his behaviour.

'But I *deliberately* didn't look round. I knew it was you. I recognized your carriage when you drove up to the house. So I went down to the beach.'

'To get away from me as far as you could?'

She repeated softly, 'To get away from you as far as I could.'

He laughed again. 'Well, you see it's no use. I may as well tell you that I came here to find you. And I *have* found you. But look here, we must start or we'll miss our boat.'

They went back to the hotel, so that Madame Olenska could leave a note for the messenger. While Newland waited for her, he watched the stream of people passing in and out of the hotel. 'They all look so like each other,' he thought. And then suddenly came a face which was different from the rest – the face of a young man, pale with heat, or worry, or both. 'Probably a foreign businessman,' thought Newland, and then forgot about him.

When she came out, they took a taxi to the harbour, and were soon on a boat moving smoothly out into the open sea. As they left the city behind them, it seemed to Newland they were leaving their old familiar world behind as well. Were they starting on some voyage from which they might never return? He was afraid to ask Madame Olenska if she felt the same – she trusted him to remain calm and not speak of his feelings. There had been days and nights when the memory of their kiss had burned on his lips, and the thought of her had run through him like fire. But now that she was beside him, they seemed to have reached the kind of deeper nearness that a touch or a word might destroy.

When they arrived at Point Arley, the hotel dining room was

full of a noisy party of school-teachers on holiday, so Newland asked for a private room, with a view over the sea. There he and Madame Olenska sat down to their lunch, like two old friends who had so much to say to each other . . .

They talked of all that had happened in the year and a half since they had met. They talked of ideas and social changes, the narrow minds of New Yorkers, and the reasons why she had decided to move to Washington.

'There are more varieties of people and of opinion there,' she said. 'Our New York friends seem to follow blindly the old ideas from England. But it seems stupid to have discovered America only to make it into a copy of another country.'

'Ah, it's what I've always told you,' said Newland sadly. 'You don't like us. We're dull. We've no character, no colour. I wonder,' he broke out, 'why you don't go back to him?'

Her eyes darkened, and he expected an angry reply. But she sat in silent thought, and he grew frightened that she might answer that she wondered too.

At last she said, 'I believe it's because of you.'

Newland reddened, but dared not move or speak.

'At least,' she continued, 'it was you who made me understand that under the dullness there are things so fine and sensitive that even those I most cared for in my other life look cheap by comparison. For a long time I've hoped this chance would come – so that I could tell you how you've helped me, what you've made of me . . .'

Newland broke in with a laugh. 'And what do you think you've made of *me*? I'm the man who married one woman because another woman told him to.'

'I thought – you promised – not to say such things!'

'Ah – how like a woman! None of you will accept a bad situation, or do anything about it!'

'*Is* it a bad situation – for May?' she asked in a low voice. 'Because that's what we've always got to think of, isn't it? That's what you've shown me.'

'I've shown you?' he echoed, looking blindly out at the sea.

'If it's not worthwhile,' she said painfully, 'to have given up our wishes, to save other people from misery, then everything I came home for, everything you've taught me, everything that

'I believe it's because of you,' said Ellen Olenska.

makes my other life look so poor because no one there bothers about it – all these things are a pretence or a dream . . .'

'And if it's not worthwhile,' he finished for her, 'there's no reason on earth why you shouldn't go back?'

Her eyes stared desperately into his. 'Oh, *is* there no reason?'

'Not if you were hoping for the success of my marriage,' he said fiercely. 'My marriage is certainly not worth staying for. Well, what do you expect? You let me see a real life, just for a moment, and at the same time asked me to go on with a false one. It's more than any human being can bear – that's all.'

'Oh, don't say that – when I'm bearing it!' she burst out, her eyes filling with tears.

Newland sat dumbly, staring at her. 'You too – oh, all this time, you too?' She did not answer, but let the tears run down her face. He was thinking, with a strange sort of happiness, 'Now I shall never again feel completely alone.'

But after a moment he was in despair again. There they were, close together, yet so tied to their separate lives that they might as well be half a world apart.

'What's the use – when you will go back?' he cried out.

She sat without moving. 'Oh, I won't go yet!'

'Not yet? Some time, then? Some time in the future?'

At that she gave him her clearest look. 'I promise you, not as long as you can bear it. Not as long as we can look straight at each other like this.'

He turned to look out at the sea again. What her answer really said was, 'If you lift a finger, you'll drive me back to all the horrors you know of, and all the temptations you half guess.' The thought kept him to his side of the table, safely away from her.

'What a life for you!' he cried.

'Oh, it's bearable – as long as it's a part of yours.'

'And as long as mine's a part of yours?'

'Yes.'

'And that's to be all – for either of us?'

'Well, it *is* all, isn't it?'

At that he jumped up, forgetting everything but the sweetness of her face. She stood up too, and their hands met. They stood in that way for a long time, looking deep into each other's eyes, reading each other's hearts.

'Don't – don't be unhappy,' she said, with a break in her voice, as she drew her hands away.

And he answered, 'You won't go back – you won't go back?'

'I won't go back,' she said.

In silence they took the boat back to Boston harbour, and Newland left Madame Olenska at the Parker House Hotel.

The next morning he arrived back in New York, to start work again, as he had told May he would do. Although he had not even managed to kiss Madame Olenska's hand or persuade her to meet him again, he felt surprisingly calm. He realized he must not tempt her to come closer to him, or she would simply return to her husband. He was determined to wait, and trust her to decide when they could meet again.

On the way to his office he recognized the young man that he had seen coming out of the Parker House Hotel. The man recognized him at the same moment, and came over to shake his hand.

'Surely, Monsieur, we met at the Carfrys'?' said the foreigner.

'Ah, yes! Monsieur Rivière!' said Newland. 'What are you doing in New York? Come and have lunch with me.'

The young Frenchman thanked him, but asked if he could instead call on Newland at his office that afternoon. They agreed a time, and Newland gave him directions.

When Monsieur Rivière arrived, he looked pale and serious. He explained that he had been sent to Boston with a message from his employer for the Countess Olenska.

The blood rushed to Newland's face. 'In other words, you are Count Olenski's messenger?'

'That is true, but this is my own message I am bringing you. You may not know, Monsieur, that Madame Olenska's family are trying to persuade her to return to her husband.'

'Good God!' cried Newland. He sat in silent shock, realizing he had been cut out of the family's discussions. Somehow, they must know he was no longer on their side. He remembered May saying recently that Ellen might be happier with her husband, and his angry reply. May had not spoken Ellen's name since then.

He stared at the Frenchman. 'I didn't know,' he said.

'Exactly, Monsieur. And I beg you . . . I beg you – Don't let her go back!' The Frenchman spoke with desperate sincerity.

'May I ask if you advised the Countess not to go back?'

The Frenchman reddened. 'No, Monsieur, I gave her the Count's message as I had been ordered to do. But after talking to her, I realized that she has changed. Monsieur, her life with him now would be unbearable. I worked for the Count for many years, and returned to his employment only recently – but I promise you, I shall never work for him again!'

'Thank you,' said Newland simply. Both men were very moved. They shook hands, and Monsieur Rivière left the office.

CHAPTER 8
THE BEAUFORT SCANDAL

In November of that same year, Mrs Archer gave a dinner party. Janey, Newland and May were there, with Sillerton Jackson and his sister Sophy. Their first subject of conversation was Julius Beaufort's financial situation. His business was failing rapidly, and what was worse, it appeared that he had taken unlawful steps to try to solve his problems.

'Poor cousin Regina!' said Mrs Archer sadly. No one really liked Beaufort, and it was almost a pleasure to think the worst of his private life, but the idea of his bringing dishonour on his wife's family was too shocking for even his enemies to enjoy. Nothing could save Regina Beaufort from social ruin, if there were any truth in the reports of her husband's misbehaviour.

The talk then turned to Mrs Struthers' musical evenings, which by now had become acceptable to much of New York society – though not yet to Mrs Archer. Shaking her head, this lady said to May, 'You know, dear, I've never quite forgiven your cousin Ellen for being the first to attend her Sunday evenings.'

May blushed, and said quietly, 'Oh, *Ellen* – well, what can you expect? She's lived abroad – and she doesn't care about society. In fact, I'm not sure what she *does* care about.'

Everyone knew that Countess Olenska's family disapproved very strongly of her refusal to return to her husband. After all, a young woman's place was under her husband's roof, especially if she had left it in a way that . . . well . . . if one looked into it . . .

Soon the ladies left the gentlemen alone with their cigars, and Sillerton Jackson said to Newland, 'If Beaufort is ruined, there'll be some unpleasant discoveries. He hasn't spent all his money on Regina, you know.'

Newland was not paying attention. He was wondering why May had blushed at the mention of Ellen's name. It was four months since the midsummer day he had spent with Ellen in Boston. He had not seen her since, and she had become the centre of his secret thoughts and hopes. He had written to her once, asking when they were to meet again, and she had replied with two words: 'Not yet.'

He became aware that Mr Jackson was speaking again. 'It's certainly a pity that Madame Olenska refused to accept her husband's latest offer.'

'A pity? In God's name, why?'

'Well, what's she going to live on, if Beaufort—'

Newland jumped up and banged his hand down angrily on the table. 'What do you mean by that, sir? Explain yourself!'

Mr Jackson spoke calmly, but his sharp little eyes were watching Newland's face with interest.

'Well, my dear boy, old Mrs Mingott tells me the Countess is no longer given much of an income by the family. And the few savings Medora Manson has left are all in Beaufort's hands, so if it comes to a crash, she'll lose everything. So what the two women will live on then, I can't imagine.'

Newland, aware that in his anger he might say something unwise, changed the subject, and took Mr Jackson up to join the ladies in the sitting room.

That evening, when they were at home in their sitting room, he watched May bending over a lamp to light it. 'How young she is!' he thought; and then, with a kind of horror, 'how young we both are! For what endless years this life will have to go on!'

'Look here,' he said, 'I may have to go to Washington next week, on business. There's an important court case coming up.'

She thought for a moment, and then smiled at him. 'The change will do you good,' she said, 'and you must see Ellen.' She looked him straight in the eyes with her cloudless smile.

Those were the only words that passed between them on the subject, but in the unspoken language which they had both been trained to use, that meant: 'I support my family's efforts to persuade Ellen to return to her husband. For some reason you have chosen not to tell me, you have advised her against this, and because of your advice, there is a great deal of unpleasant talk about her behaviour. I know you intend to see Ellen when you're in Washington – perhaps you're even going there in order to see her. I am giving you my full permission to see her – I want you to let her know what will happen if she continues to go against her family's wishes.'

She moved towards the door. 'I am going to bed, dear,' she said. At the door she turned and paused for his kiss.

The crash came a few days later. With false confidence Beaufort had persuaded a large number of people that his bank was safe, and money had poured in. But it had not been enough to pay his enormous debts, and he was ruined. So, too, were many of the people who had trusted him, and ugly things were being said of his wicked behaviour. It was one of the worst financial scandals in the history of Wall Street.

While Mr Letterblair was telling Newland the details of the disaster, a note was delivered to the young man. It said:

*Please come to Grandmother's house as soon as possible. She
has had a stroke – somehow she heard this awful news about
the bank before anyone else. Uncle Lovell is away shooting,
and the idea of the dishonour has made poor Father ill, so
he can't leave his room. Mother and I need you very badly.*
May

At Mrs Mingott's house Newland found his wife and her
mother looking pale and worried. The doctor, however, was
quite hopeful and the old lady's determination to get well soon
began to have an effect on her relations.

It appeared that on the previous evening Regina Beaufort had
come to visit Mrs Mingott, and begged her aunt to support her
and her husband in their desperate situation. This request had
made Mrs Mingott extremely angry. When she was able to speak
again, she told her daughter Mrs Welland what had been said.

'I said to Regina, "Honour's always been honour, and
honesty's always been honesty in this house, and will be until
I'm carried out of it feet first." And when she said, "But I'm
your niece!" I said, "You were Beaufort's wife when he covered
you with jewels, and you'll have to stay Beaufort's wife now
that he's covered you with dirt."'

Anger had probably caused Mrs Mingott's stroke, and Mrs
Welland and May were horrified at Regina's behaviour. Everyone
knew that a wife should not ask her family to cover up her
husband's financial dishonour; a wife simply had to accept the
rough as well as the smooth, the bad times as well as the good.

As they sat discussing it all, a servant called Mrs Welland into
Mrs Mingott's room. She came out again a few minutes later,
looking annoyed. 'She wants me to send a telegram to Ellen
Olenska. She wants her here at once,' she said.

There was a moment's silence. 'I suppose it must be done,' she added doubtfully.

'Of course it must be done,' said May. 'We must carry out Grandmother's wishes.' She turned to Newland with a smile. 'Will *you* send the telegram for us, Newland? There's just time before lunch.'

She sat down and wrote the telegram. As she handed it to him, she said, smiling, 'What a pity! This means you will miss Ellen.' Turning to her mother, she explained, 'Newland has to go to Washington for a court case, and now the doctor tells us Grandmother will live, it doesn't seem right to ask him to give up such important business in order to stay here, does it?'

Mrs Welland replied quickly, 'Of course not, dearest. Your grandmother would be the last person to wish it.'

As Newland left the room with the telegram, he heard his mother-in-law add, 'But why does she want Ellen here?' and May's clear voice reply, 'Perhaps to explain to her again that her duty is with her husband.'

That afternoon the announcement of the Beaufort failure was in all the newspapers. The whole of New York was darkened by the story of Beaufort's dishonour – he had not only lied to people about the safety of their savings, but his bank had continued to take in money for twenty-four hours after its failure was certain. And no one pitied his wife, because she did not seem to understand the seriousness of his crimes, but talked of the disaster as 'a misfortune' and was sure that 'her true friends would not desert her'. Her true friends were sure they would.

Old Mrs Mingott continued to get better, and gave orders that no one should ever mention the name of Beaufort to her again.

The next day the Wellands received a telegram, announcing Madame Olenska's arrival from Washington the following evening. This started a long discussion at the Wellands', where Newland and May were having lunch, about who could meet Ellen at Jersey City railway station. Mr and Mrs Welland were visiting Mrs Mingott that afternoon, the Lovell Mingotts were busy, and May could not be asked to travel so far alone.

Newland, becoming aware of their discussion, said, 'Shall I fetch her? I can easily get away from the office, and I can take May's carriage.' His heart was beating excitedly as he spoke.

'Oh, thank you so much, Newland!' said Mrs Welland gratefully, and May smiled at him, pleased.

May's carriage was waiting outside, for her to drive Newland back to the office after lunch. As they got in and sat down, she said, 'I didn't want to worry Mother, but how can you meet Ellen tomorrow, when you're going to Washington?'

'Oh, I'm not going,' said Newland.

'Not going? Why, what's happened?' Her voice was as clear as a bell, and full of wifely concern.

'The case has been put off for a few weeks.'

'Put off? How odd! I heard from Mother that Mr Letterblair is going to Washington tomorrow, to defend a case.'

'Well – that's it. The whole office can't go.'

'Then it hasn't been put off?' she continued, with an insistence so unusual that he blushed for her.

'No, but my going *has* been,' he answered. It did not hurt him half as much to tell May a lie, as to see her trying to pretend she had not discovered it.

'I'm not going until later on, luckily for the convenience of your family,' he said. As he spoke, he felt she was looking at him, and he turned his eyes to hers in order not to appear to be avoiding them. Their eyes met for a second, and perhaps they saw more deeply into each other's meaning than either of them really wanted . . .

'Yes, it is awfully convenient,' May brightly agreed, 'that you can meet Ellen after all. You saw how pleased Mother was.'

'Oh, I'm delighted to do it.' The carriage stopped at his office, and as he jumped out, she laid her hand on his. 'Goodbye, dearest,' she said, her eyes so blue that he wondered afterwards if they had shone on him through tears.

He turned and hurried into his office, repeating to himself in a sort of song, 'It's all of two hours from Jersey City station to Mrs Mingott's! It's all of two hours – and it may be more!'

May laid her hand on Newland's. 'Goodbye, dearest,' she said.

CHAPTER 9
ELLEN RETURNS TO NEW YORK

The following evening Newland was waiting at Jersey City station for the Washington train. In his senseless schoolboy happiness he pictured Madame Olenska getting out of the train, then her arm in his as he guided her to the carriage, and then a journey that would go on for ever. He had so much to say to her!

The train came in, and he saw her pale face in the crowd of passengers. They reached each other, their hands met, and he drew her arm through his. 'This way – I have the carriage,' he said. After that it all happened as he had dreamed.

'Do you know,' he said, as they drove away from the station, 'I almost couldn't remember you? How can I explain? *Each time you happen to me all over again.*'

'Oh, yes, I know! I know! It happens to me too!'

'Ellen – Ellen – Ellen!'

She made no answer and he sat in silence, watching her as she looked out of the window. How little they knew of each other, after all! The precious moments were slipping away, but he had forgotten everything he meant to say.

'What a pretty carriage!' she said, suddenly turning her face from the window. 'Is it May's? She sent you to fetch me, then? How kind of her!'

Her mentioning May's name made him angry, so he burst out, 'Your husband's secretary came to see me, you know.'

'I'm not surprised. He'd met you in England, hadn't he?'

'Ellen – I must ask you one thing. Was it Rivière who helped you to get away – when you left your husband?'

'Yes. I owe him a great debt,' she replied calmly.

'I think you're the most honest woman I ever met!'

'Oh no – but probably one of the least difficult.'

'Well – you've had to look at things as they are.'

'Yes – I've had to look at wickedness, it's true.'

'It hasn't blinded you!'

'It doesn't blind one, but it dries up one's tears.'

The answer seemed to come from depths of experience beyond Newland's reach.

'If you're not blind, then, you must see this can't last,' he said. 'Our being together – and not together.'

'No. You shouldn't have come today,' and suddenly she turned, threw her arms around him and pressed her lips to his. In a moment she drew away, and they sat silent and unmoving, until Newland started speaking hurriedly.

'Don't be afraid of me. A stolen kiss isn't what I want. Look, I'm not even trying to touch your sleeve. When we're apart, and I'm looking forward to seeing you, every thought is burnt up in a great flame. But then you come and you're so much more than I remembered, and what I want of you is so much more than an hour or two, with weeks of thirsty waiting between, that I can sit perfectly still beside you like this, just quietly trusting my dream to come true.'

For a moment she was silent. 'What do you mean by trusting it to come true?' she whispered.

'Why – you know it will, don't you?'

'Your dream of you and me together?' She burst into a sudden hard laugh. 'You choose a good place to tell me about it!'

'You mean, in my wife's carriage? Shall we get out and walk? I don't suppose you mind a little snow?'

She laughed again, more quietly. 'No, I don't want to walk, because I want to see my grandmother as soon as possible. We'll sit quietly, and we'll look, not at dreams, but at realities.'

'The only reality for me is this.'

There was a long silence. 'Is it your idea, then, that I should live with you as your mistress, since I can't be your wife?'

He was shocked by her plain speaking, and had difficulty finding the words. 'I want – I want to get away to a place where we could simply be two human beings who love each other, who are the whole of life to each other, and nothing else will matter.'

She laughed. 'Oh my dear – where is that country? Have you ever been there? Believe me, it's a miserable little place!'

'Then what exactly is your plan for us?' cried Newland.

'For *us*? But there's no *us* in that sense! We're only Newland Archer, husband of Ellen Olenska's cousin, and Ellen Olenska, cousin of Newland Archer's wife, trying to be happy behind the backs of the people who trust them.'

'Ah, I'm beyond that,' whispered Newland.

'No, you're not! You've never been beyond. And *I* have,' she said in a strange voice, 'and I know what it looks like there.'

He sat silent, in wordless pain. Then he rang the bell to tell the driver to stop. 'I'll get out here,' he said, opening the door and jumping out. 'You're right, I shouldn't have come.' She bent forward, about to speak, but he had already called out the order to drive on. As the carriage rolled away, he felt something stiff and cold on his face, and realized that he had been crying, and the icy wind had frozen his tears.

That evening Newland had dinner at home with May, who did not mention Ellen Olenska once. After dinner they sat together in the sitting room. May was doing her sewing, while Newland was reading. Occasionally he raised his eyes from his book and looked at May with secret despair. He would always know her thoughts; never would she surprise him by an unexpected mood or a new idea. Now she was simply becoming a copy of her mother, and mysteriously, in the same way, trying to turn him into a Mr Welland. He stood up impatiently, and at once she looked up.

'What's the matter, dear?'

'The room's too warm. I want a little air.' He pulled the heavy curtains and opened a window, so that he could put his head and shoulders out into the icy darkness.

'Newland! Do shut the window. You'll catch your death.'

'Catch my death!' he echoed, and felt like adding, 'I've caught it already. I *am* dead – I've been dead for months now.'

As he walked back to his chair, he laid a hand on her hair. 'Poor May!' he said.

'Poor? Why poor?' she asked with a little laugh.

'Because I shall never be able to open a window without worrying you,' he replied, also laughing.

For a moment she was silent. Then she said very low, her head bent over her sewing, 'I shall never worry if you're happy.'

'Ah, my dear! And I shall never be happy unless I can open the window!'

'In *this* weather?' she said. Without replying he buried his head in his book again.

Six or seven days passed. Newland heard nothing from Madame Olenska and became aware that her name would not be mentioned in his presence by the family. He did not try to see her, but a plan was slowly taking shape in the back of his mind.

Then one day May told him her grandmother wanted to see him, and Newland hurried over to Mrs Mingott's house. His plan was simple. He would see Ellen there and find out on which day and by which train she was returning to Washington. He would join her on that train, and travel with her, as far as she wanted to go – his choice would be Japan. He would leave a note for May that would prevent his ever coming back.

But old Mrs Mingott told him with great delight that she had managed to persuade Ellen to stay in New York and look after her. Newland felt confused. He would be able to see Ellen now and then, but their future would be limited to secret meetings and letters. He would find himself telling more lies to May, and going against habit and honour and all the ancient rules he and his people had always believed in . . .

As he was walking down Fifth Avenue, he saw Mrs Mingott's carriage outside the Beauforts' house, and knew Ellen must be visiting Regina Beaufort. He waited, and stopped Ellen as she was coming out of the front door.

'I must see you tomorrow – somewhere we can be alone,' he said. 'At the Museum of Art, in the park? At half-past two?'

She turned away without replying, and got quickly into the carriage. 'She'll be there!' he told himself confidently.

In the Museum of Art they walked slowly through the rooms. There were no other visitors, and their steps echoed loudly.

'It's a strange place,' said Madame Olenska.

'Some day, I suppose it'll be a great museum.'

He sat down and watched the light movements of her figure,

so girlish even under her heavy furs, as she looked at the paintings.

'What is it you wanted to tell me?' she asked.

'I believe you came to New York because you were afraid of my coming to Washington. Did you know I was planning to?'

She looked down. 'Well – yes. I knew.'

'Well, then?' he insisted.

'Well, then. This is better, isn't it? We shall hurt others less. Isn't it, after all, what you always wanted?'

'To meet you in this way, in secret? It's the opposite of what I want. I think it's horrible!'

'Oh, I'm so glad! So do I!' she cried out.

'Then, what is it, in God's name, that you think is better?'

Instead of answering, she whispered, 'I promised to stay with Grandmother, because I thought I'd be safer here.'

'Safer from me? Safer from loving me?'

'Safer from harming other people.' She looked at him with a kind of terror, and blushed. 'Shall I – once come to you, and then go home?' she suddenly said in a low clear voice.

'Dearest!' said Newland, the blood rushing to his forehead. 'But what do you mean by going home?'

'Home to my husband.'

'And you expect me to say yes to that?'

'What else is there? I can't stay here and lie to the people who've been good to me. I can't go away with you and destroy their lives, when they've helped me to remake mine.' She turned away. 'I must go,' she said.

He followed, and caught her hand. 'Well, then, come to me once,' he said, unable to bear the thought of losing her. 'When?' he insisted. 'Tomorrow?'

She hesitated. 'The day after.'

'Dearest!' he said again. For a moment they continued to look into each other's eyes, and he saw that her face, even paler now, was flooded with a deep inner happiness. Then she walked hurriedly away, turning in the doorway to wave goodbye.

The next evening Newland and May went to the opera, as guests of the van der Luydens. The Swedish singer Christine Nilsson was singing in *Faust*, just as she had done two years before, when Newland had first seen Ellen in her grandmother's box. Tonight Newland had moved to sit with some of his men friends, and from here he had a good view of his wife as she sat in the van der Luydens' box.

'How innocent and trusting she looks!' he thought. He remembered how nobly she had once offered to give him up, and suddenly he decided to tell her the truth, to throw himself on her generosity, and ask for the freedom he had once refused.

He got up and walked round the theatre, slipping into the back of the van der Luydens' box. 'I've got a bad headache,' he whispered to May. 'Will you come home with me?'

May said a few words to her mother and Mrs van der Luyden, and soon she and Newland were driving home.

They went into their sitting room together. 'Hadn't you better go to bed at once?' she asked anxiously.

'My head's not as bad as that,' Newland replied. 'There's something important I want to say to you – about myself.'

She sat silent, looking extremely pale, but calm.

'Madame Olenska—' he said, but his wife raised her hand to stop him. The gaslight shone on her gold wedding ring.

'Oh, why should we talk about Ellen tonight? Is it really

worthwhile, dear? You've understood her, no doubt, better than we all did; you've always been kind to her. But what does it matter, now it's all over?'

'All over – what do you mean?'

'Why – she's going back to Europe. Grandmother agrees, and has arranged to make her independent of her husband.'

Newland turned away and covered his face. May sat without moving or speaking. At last he turned back to her.

'It's impossible,' he said. 'How do you know that?'

'I saw Ellen yesterday – at Grandmother's. And I had a note from her this afternoon. Do you want to see it?'

He could not find his voice. She handed him a short letter, which Newland took with a trembling hand and read. It said:

May dear, I have at last made Grandmother see that if I return to Europe, I must live by myself – she has been as kind and generous as ever. I am going back to Washington to pack, and I sail from New York next week, with poor Aunt Medora. If any of my friends want to try to change my mind, please tell them it would be useless. Ellen

Newland burst out laughing wildly. 'Why did she write this?' he asked.

May looked at him with her clear blue eyes. 'I suppose because we talked things over yesterday. I told her I understood how hard it had been for her here. I knew you'd been the one friend she had always felt sure of, and I wanted her to know that you and I were the same – in all our feelings.' She added slowly, 'She understood my wishing to tell her this. I think she understands everything.'

She went up to Newland, and taking one of his cold hands, pressed it quickly to her face. 'My head aches too. Good night, dear,' she said, and turned to the door.

It was, as Mrs Archer smilingly said to Mrs Welland, a great event for a young couple to give their first big dinner. It had been May's idea to give a dinner for Ellen, the evening before she sailed for Europe. Now, as Newland looked round at the familiar faces at his table – May, the van der Luydens, Lawrence Lefferts, Sillerton and Sophy Jackson, the Lovell Mingotts, and Ellen – he began to realize that New York society almost certainly thought he and Ellen were lovers, but they were pretending his was a wonderfully happy marriage. And now that Ellen was leaving, it was easy for them all to pretend that they admired and respected her. He hated this dishonesty, and began to feel like a prisoner, constantly guarded by his friends and relations.

He could not remember what he said to anyone during dinner, and soon it was time for his guests to leave. There had been no chance to speak privately to Ellen. 'Goodbye,' he said to her in the hall, as he helped her on with her coat. 'But I shall see you soon in Paris.' His voice sounded loud in his ears.

'Oh,' she whispered, 'if you and May could come . . .!'

And then she was getting into the van der Luydens' carriage, and he could no longer see her face.

A few minutes later May came to find him in the library. 'It *did* go well, didn't it?' she said.

Newland made an effort to speak. 'Now that you're here, there's something I must tell you. I tried to, the other night.'

'Yes, dear. Something about yourself?'

'Yes. I've been horribly tired lately—'

'Oh, I've seen it coming on, Newland! You've been so wickedly overworked at the office!'

'Perhaps it's that. Anyway, I want to make a break – to go away at once. On a long trip, away from everything—'

'A long trip? Where, for example?'

'Oh, I don't know, India – or Japan.'

She stood up, and came nearer to his chair.

'As far as that? But I'm afraid you can't, dear.' Her voice trembled a little. 'Not unless you take me with you. That is, if

'But I'm afraid you can't, dear,' said May. 'Not unless you take me with you.'

83

the doctors will let me go . . . but I'm afraid they won't. You see, Newland, I've been sure since this morning of something I've been hoping for so much . . .'

He stared up at her, his face deathly white, and she knelt down to hide her face against his knee.

'Oh, my dear,' he said, with his cold hand on her hair. There was a devilish kind of laughter inside his head.

'You didn't guess?' asked May.

'Yes – I – no. That is, of course, I hoped . . .' They looked at each other for a moment and again fell silent. 'Have you told anyone else?' he added.

'Only my mother and yours.' She paused, blushing. 'And Ellen. You know I told you I'd had a long talk with her one afternoon?'

'Ah . . .' said Newland, his heart stopping.

He felt that his wife was watching him closely. 'Did you *mind* my telling her first, Newland?'

'Mind? Why should I?' He made a last effort to think clearly. 'But that was a fortnight ago, wasn't it? I thought you said you weren't sure till today.'

Her colour burned deeper, but she kept her eyes on his. 'No, I wasn't sure then – but I told her I was. And you see I was right!' she cried, her blue eyes wet with victory.

CHAPTER 10

NEWLAND VISITS PARIS

Newland sat at the desk in his library, and looked round at the room where most of the real things of his life had happened over the last thirty years. There his wife, nearly twenty-six years ago, had blushingly told him she was expecting a baby. There his elder son Dallas had taken his first steps towards him, shouting, 'Dad!' There his daughter Mary, who was so like her mother, had announced her engagement to the dullest of Reggie Chivers' sons. And there his great friend Theodore Roosevelt had told him, 'Forget about the professional politicians, Archer! It's men like you the country wants.'

'Men like you' – how those words had impressed Newland! How eagerly he had answered the call! At last he had found something worthwhile to do, and he worked long hours in local government. After a while, however, he felt he had done what he could, and returned thankfully to a quieter life. He was admired and respected in New York; his days were full, and they were filled usefully. 'I suppose that's all a man should ask,' he thought.

Something he knew he had missed – the flower of life. But when he thought, so despairingly at first, of Ellen Olenska, over the years she became the picture of perfection, and that picture kept him from thinking of other women. He had been a good husband to May, and when she had suddenly died – carried off by the illness through which she had nursed their youngest child,

Bill – he had honestly mourned her. Their long years together had shown him that it did not matter so much if marriage was a dull duty, as long as the couple always behaved in a responsible, dutiful way to each other. If they failed to do that, the marriage just became a battle of selfish interests. Thinking back over his life, he saw there was honour in his past, and he mourned for it. After all, there was good in the old ways.

His eyes rested on his first photograph of May, which still kept its place on his desk. There she was, just as he had seen her under the Florida orange trees. And she had remained the same – never quite as noble as on that day, but never far below – brave, generous, trusting, but with so little imagination that the world of her childhood had fallen into pieces and rebuilt itself without her noticing the changes. Her children protected her by hiding their modern opinions from her, as Newland hid his. And she died thinking the world a good place, full of happy, loving families like her own; she could bear to leave it because she trusted that, whatever happened, Newland would continue teaching Dallas to obey the same rules that *he* had been taught, and that Dallas (when Newland followed her) would do the same for little Bill. Of Mary she was as sure as of her own self. So, having saved little Bill from death, and given her life in the effort, she went happily to her place in the Archer family grave.

The telephone rang, and Newland answered it. How far they were from the days when a messenger boy was the fastest way of communicating!

'Chicago wants you.'

Ah, it must be Dallas, who was there on business for his firm.

'Hallo, Dad. Yes, Dallas here. I say – how do you feel about sailing to France on Wednesday on the *Mauretania*? I've got to

be back in early June for my wedding' – the voice broke into a
laugh – 'so we must hurry. I say, Dad, do come. Think it over?
No, sir, not for a minute. If you can find a single reason why
not – no, I knew you couldn't. Oh good! I knew you'd agree.'

It would be their last trip together, because in June Dallas was
marrying Fanny Beaufort – she was Julius Beaufort's daughter
by his second wife, Fanny Ring, the mistress he had married after
poor Regina died. It was tempting for Newland to take this last
chance of being alone with his first-born son. And France! He
had not been there since his honeymoon. May had disliked
travelling, and preferred the conversation of friends and family
to that of foreigners.

Since her death, nearly two years before, there had been no
reason for Newland to continue in the same routine. But the
worst of doing his duty was that it had made him unable to
do anything else. There are moments, however, when a man's
imagination suddenly rises above its daily level, and looks down
over all the crossroads and turning points in the long road of
life. Newland hung there and wondered . . .

Looking out of his hotel window at the streets of Paris in the
spring sunshine, he felt his heart beating with a young man's
confusion and eagerness. In the first impatient years he had often
imagined the scene of his victorious return to Paris and Ellen,
but now that he was here, he felt shy, old-fashioned, dull – just
a grey shadow of a man compared with the brilliant figure he
had dreamed of being . . .

Dallas's hand came down cheerfully on his shoulder. 'Hallo,
Father, this is wonderful, isn't it?' They stood for a while, and
then the young man continued, 'By the way, I've got a message

for you: the Countess Olenska expects us both at half-past five.'

He spoke lightly, carelessly, but turning to look at him, Newland thought he could see a knowing smile in his eyes.

'Didn't I tell you?' Dallas went on. 'Fanny made me promise to see Madame Olenska. She was awfully good to Fanny as a little girl, when Mr Beaufort sent Fanny over to France from Argentina. Fanny didn't have any friends, and Madame Olenska was very kind to her. So I telephoned today and asked to see her.'

Newland stared at him. 'You told her I was here?'

'Of course – why not?' Dallas slipped his arm through his father's. 'I say, Father, what was she like? Confess – you and she were great friends, weren't you? Wasn't she awfully lovely?'

'Lovely? I don't know about that. She was *different*.'

'Ah – there you have it! She's different, and one doesn't know why. It's exactly what I feel about Fanny.'

His father looked shocked. 'But my dear boy – you and Fanny . . . that's quite a different situation . . .'

'Oh Dad, don't be so old-fashioned! Wasn't she – once – your Fanny? I mean, the woman you'd have given up everything for, but you didn't.'

'I didn't,' echoed Newland, frowning.

'No, dear old boy, you didn't. But Mother said – she sent for me the day before she died, you remember? She said she knew we were safe with you, and always would be, because once, when she'd asked you to, you'd given up the thing you most wanted.'

Newland received this strange communication in silence. At last he said in a low voice: 'She never asked me.'

'No, you never did ask each other anything, did you? You just sat and watched each other, and guessed at what was going on underneath. But I think you older people knew more about each other's private thoughts than we ever have time to find out about our own.'

It seemed to take an iron hand from Newland's heart to know that his wife had, after all, guessed and pitied. For a long time he looked out of the window, while the stream of life rolled by . . . 'I'm only fifty-seven!' he found himself thinking. Summer dreams were past, but surely it was not too late for a quiet autumn of friendship, with Ellen as his companion.

Together he and Dallas walked through the streets towards Madame Olenska's apartment, the son full of excited enthusiasm for Paris, the father busy with his thoughts.

More than half a lifetime divided him from Madame Olenska. She had lived in this ancient beautiful city, among people he did not know, in a rich atmosphere of theatres, and paintings, and books, and conversations he could only guess at. During all those years he had lived with his unchanging memory of her, but her memory of him might no longer be as bright as the flame he carried in his own heart.

They found the building, and looked up at the fifth floor to a balcony, and windows with pale green shutters, which were open.

'I think I'll sit down for a moment,' said Newland, pointing to a bench under some trees in the square.

'Why – aren't you well?' his son asked.

'Perfectly well. But I'd like you to go up without me.'

'But Dad, does that mean you won't come up at all?'

'I don't know,' said Newland slowly.

'But what shall I say?'

'My dear boy, don't you always know what to say?'

'Very well. I'll say you're old-fashioned, and prefer walking up the stairs because you don't like lifts.'

His father smiled. 'Just say I'm old-fashioned.'

Puzzled, Dallas shook his head and went inside.

Archer sat down on the bench, and continued to look up at the balcony and the windows with the pale green shutters. In his mind he could see Dallas entering the room with his rapid, light step, and a dark lady with a pale face, who would look up quickly and hold out a long thin hand with three rings on it.

'It's more real to me here than if I went up,' he suddenly heard himself say, and the fear of losing that last shadow of reality kept him in his seat.

He sat for a long time on the bench in the thickening darkness, his eyes never turning from the windows. At last a lamp was lit inside the apartment, and a servant closed the shutters.

At that, Newland Archer stood up slowly and walked back alone to his hotel.

GLOSSARY

admire to have a very good opinion of someone or something; **admiration** *(n)*

affair (in this story) a sexual relationship outside marriage

announce to tell people something officially; **announcement** *(n)*

atmosphere the feeling or mood that a person has in a particular place or situation

ball a formal party for dancing

bear *(v)* to suffer pain or unhappiness; **bearable** *(adj)*

best man a male friend or relative of the bridegroom who assists him at his wedding

blush *(v)* to become red in the face, especially when embarrassed

box a small seating area in a theatre separated off from where other people sit

bridegroom a man on his wedding day

bridesmaid a young woman or girl who helps a bride before and during the wedding ceremony

brilliant very bright; clever; successful

brilliantly brightly; extremely

bunch (of flowers) a number of flowers fastened together

carriage a vehicle, pulled by horses, for carrying people

court-case a criminal or legal matter which involves a trial

Count a title for a man of noble family

Countess a title for the wife of a Count

daughter-in-law your son's wife; **son-in-law** your daughter's husband

debt money that is owed to someone; a feeling of owing something to someone

despair *(n)* a feeling of hopelessness

91

disapprove to think that someone or something is bad or wrong

dishonour a loss of honour or respect because someone has done something bad or unacceptable

Duke a title for a man of the highest social position

embarrass to put people in a difficult situation, to make people feel uncomfortable

exotic seeming exciting or unusual because it is connected with foreign countries

familiar (with) knowing something very well

fiancée the woman whom a man is going to marry

financial connected with money and finance

firm *(n)* a company or business

fur the skin of an animal with the hair still on it

gentleman a man of good family who always behaves well

give up to allow someone else to have someone or something

good taste (in this story) the ability to behave in a way that society considers correct

heaven a place or situation in which people are very happy

honeymoon a holiday for a man and woman who have just got married

honour the quality of knowing and doing what is morally right

mistress a woman who is having a sexual relationship with a man she is not married to

Monsieur the French word for 'Mr' or 'sir'

mourn to feel and show sadness because someone has died

noble being courageous and honest, thinking about other people; **nobility** *(n)*

old-fashioned not modern, no longer fashionable

opera a dramatic work in which most of the words are sung to music

pure morally good; **purity** *(n)*

respect *(v)* to admire or have a high opinion of someone because of their good qualities

ribbons thin pieces of material worn on a woman's dress or hair

right *(n)* a thing that people are allowed to do or have

rule *(n)* a fixed instruction that must be obeyed

scandal behaviour or events that people think are shocking or wicked; talk or reports about someone's shocking behaviour

scene a part of a play in which the action happens in one place

shutters metal or wooden covers for windows, to keep out the heat and light

sleeve the part of a shirt, coat, etc. that covers the arm

stroke *(n)* a sudden serious illness when a blood vessel in the brain bursts

telegram a short urgent message sent by electric current along wires, and then printed and delivered

tempt to attract someone, or to make someone want to do something

temptation the desire to do something that you know is wrong

trust *(v)* to have confidence in someone

victory winning or achieving something

virgin a person who has never had sex

vulgar low, common, coarse, lacking in manners

wicked evil, of bad character

worthwhile important, valuable, useful

ACTIVITIES

Before Reading

1 **Read the back cover and the story introduction on the first page. What do you know now about the people in the story? Circle Y (Yes) or N (No) for each of these sentences.**

1 Ellen Olenska hopes to return to her husband. Y / N
2 May thinks it is important not to offend people. Y / N
3 Newland used to be in love with Ellen. Y / N

2 **This story is set in New York in the 1870s. Can you guess what kind of social rules there were in those days? Decide which of these statements might be true or not true.**

1 Divorce had to be avoided, to save a family's good name.
2 People had a duty to express their feelings openly.
3 Arriving late at social events was a fashionable thing to do.
4 It was acceptable for young unmarried women to live alone.
5 It was acceptable for married men to have affairs with women.

3 **The story begins with Newland Archer engaged to May Welland. Here are four possible developments. Choose the one that you think most likely, or the one that you would like to happen.**

1 Newland will marry May.
2 Newland will marry Ellen.
3 Newland will marry a different woman.
4 Newland will never marry.

ACTIVITIES

While Reading

Read Chapters 1 to 3. Answer these questions in two ways; first, from the point of view of New York society in the 1870s; and secondly, from the point of view of your own culture, in your own time. Are there differences between the two sets of answers?

1 Was Ellen Olenska wrong to leave her husband, the Polish Count, and come home to America?

2 At his mother's dinner, was Newland right to say that Ellen had nothing to be ashamed of?

3 Was Newland wrong to visit Ellen at her home without making sure that May knew about his visit first?

4 Was Mr van der Luyden right to warn Ellen not to accept invitations to unsuitable events like Mrs Struthers' party?

Before you read Chapter 4, can you guess which of these things Newland will do?

1 He will advise Ellen against divorce, as her family wishes.

2 He will offer Ellen his complete support, divorce or no divorce.

Read Chapters 4 to 6. Who is speaking, to whom, and what are they talking about? What do the words tell us about them?

1 'This is a very small world, compared to the one you've lived in.'

2 'But my freedom – isn't that worth it?'

3 'You could so easily have made a mistake – anyone can.'

4 'I can't love you unless I give you up.'

5 'I wonder if she would be happier with her husband, after all.'

Read Chapters 7 and 8, and try to summarize the characters' feelings by completing these sentences.

1 Ellen has been avoiding Newland because _____.
2 Newland loves Ellen more than ever and _____.
3 May must suspect that Newland is in love with Ellen but
   _____.

Before you read Chapter 9, choose some advice to offer Newland and Ellen before they meet at the station. Explain your choices.

Advice for Newland:
1 Tell Ellen you will never meet her alone again.
2 Ask Ellen to run away with you to Europe as soon as possible.
3 Persuade Ellen to stay in New York and meet you in secret.
Advice for Ellen:
4 Go back to your husband the Count.
5 Stay in New York and become Newland's mistress.
6 Tell May about your relationship with Newland.

Before you read Chapter 10, which happens more than twenty-five years later, imagine what might happen. Choose some of these ideas, or think of some of your own.

1 Newland leaves May the next day, takes the next boat for
   Europe, finds Ellen, and they stay together, unmarried, for life.
2 May dies in childbirth; Ellen returns, and marries Newland.
3 Some years later Ellen returns to New York and wants to have
   an affair with Newland, but he is no longer interested.
4 Newland stays with May, and never sees Ellen again.
5 A year later, Newland leaves May and joins Ellen in Europe,
   but their life together is bitter and unhappy.

After Reading

1 **Read these sentences about, or said by, Newland, Ellen, and May. Explain what you think they mean. What, in your opinion, do the sentences tell us about the attitudes of these characters?**

   1 Newland: It was his duty to hide his past from her, and her duty, as a marriageable girl, to have no past to hide.

   2 Ellen: 'The real loneliness is living among all these kind people who only ask me to pretend!'

   3 May: 'Mother would not understand us wanting to do things so differently from other couples.'

2 **Here is May's diary, for the day after her grandmother's stroke. Choose one suitable word to fill each gap.**

Now I know, there is no _____ he loves her. He looked so _____ at lunch today (the way he _____ to look when we were first _____), when he offered to take my _____ and pick her up from the _____ , and poor Mother (she would be _____ if she knew!) accepted so very _____ . Then of course he had to _____ to me – he has done that _____ , but this time it seemed much _____ somehow. I do wonder if he _____ how completely I understand him, and _____ him as well, for the awful _____ that I can see he is _____ . Does he know how much I _____ him, in spite of everything? I'll _____ give him up, unless he himself _____ to leave me. I can only _____ that one day his heart will _____ to me. He is so very _____ to me.

3 Here are the thoughts of five characters from the story. Who are the characters, and who or what are they thinking about? What has just happened in the story?

1 'There'll be trouble if he gets involved with that foreign girl – most unsuitable, she is. I've seen the signs before in young men – losing their temper, not wanting a word said against the lady, talking all that nonsense about divorce. Ah well. I think I'll just have another of his cigars before I go.'

2 'Oho! Now there's a lovely-looking woman, just entering old Mrs Mingott's box. Everybody's looking at her. Who can she be? I'll get Regina to find out. I like a low-cut dress – why hide what you've got, that's what I say. She looks a lot more fun than half the women here tonight.'

3 'Oh, I'm so excited! It's such wonderful news! I'll never get to sleep again now. She's a delightful girl, just right for Newland – I'm sure they'll be happy together. But I can't understand why he was laughing like that. It was almost uncontrollable. I'm surprised he didn't wake Mother . . .'

4 'That's no way for a niece of mine to behave. There'll be no helping hand from me, that's for sure, and I don't want to hear her name spoken in this house again! Brought me close to death, she has, she and that wicked husband of hers!'

5 'It's lovely to have him here with us, and it's nice to see that he's so much in love, but I don't think he has any idea how much there is to *do* before a wedding. There are still all the sheets and towels to sew, and May's dress – so many preparations to make. I'm afraid he'll just have to wait . . .'

4 **When May talks to Ellen about Newland (see page 81), she also tells her she is expecting a child. A fortnight later she reports this conversation to Newland (see page 84). Complete what May and Ellen say to each other in this conversation.**

MAY: Ellen dear, there's something _____.

ELLEN: What is it, May? Sit down beside me and _____.

MAY: Ellen, ever since you returned to New York, I know what a difficult time _____.

ELLEN: Yes, it hasn't _____. I'm not sure I'll ever understand _____.

MAY: We New Yorkers *are* rather different _____. And you have been _____.

ELLEN: Yes, a very long time. And I am so grateful to _____.

MAY: He's very fond _____.

ELLEN: And I am of him. He's the one friend I _____.

MAY: I know that, and I've been glad that he _____. Of course, in the future he'll have other, family responsibilities, so he may not _____.

ELLEN: Family . . .? Do you mean, dear May, that _____?

MAY: Yes, I am. And Newland will _____!

ELLEN: Yes, I'm sure he will be. He doesn't _____?

MAY: Not yet. I'll tell him very soon. But I wanted you _____.

ELLEN: Yes, thank you for telling me, May. I'm so pleased _____. It's _____.

MAY: And what _____?

ELLEN: My plans? Oh, I – well, I think I will _____. I hope to persuade Grandmother to _____.

MAY: I'm sure, if you explain, Grandmother will _____.

ELLEN: I hope so, May – indeed, I do hope so . . .

5 **Which of these statements from the story do you agree or disagree with? Give your reasons.**

  1 It's better not to try to turn a dream from the past into reality.
  2 Women ought to be free, as free as men.
  3 It doesn't matter if a marriage is dull, as long as the couple respect each other.
  4 When two people love each other, they may have to go against public opinion.
  5 Sometimes you have to give up your own wishes, to save other people from misery.
  6 A wife simply has to accept the rough as well as the smooth, the bad times as well as the good.

6 **What did you think of this story? Think about these questions and how you would answer them, and write a short report of the story.**

  1 In every love triangle, there are always winners and losers. In this story, who were the winners and who were the losers, in your opinion?
  2 Was Newland right to marry May, when he was already in love with Ellen?
  3 When May offered Newland his freedom, should he have broken his engagement, and run away with Ellen?
  4 How did you find the ending? Did you feel it was satisfying, unexpected, disappointing? Describe your reaction.

ABOUT THE AUTHOR

Edith Wharton was born Edith Newbold Jones in 1862 in New York. Her family was wealthy, and very much part of New York's fashionable society. Edith was taught privately at home, where she also spent many hours reading in her father's library. In 1885 she married Edward Wharton, but their marriage was not a happy one. They divorced in 1913.

By 1907 Edith Wharton was living in France, first in Paris, which she loved, and later, in homes near Paris and on the Mediterranean coast. In the First World War (1914–1918) she did a lot to help people who were poor and homeless because of the invading enemy; for this the French government gave her the cross of the Legion of Honour. She died in the south of France in 1937.

Her first book, *The Decoration of Houses* (1897), was non-fiction, but this was followed by short stories and novels, including her first popular success, *The House of Mirth*, in 1905. She went on to write more than forty books, including *Ethan Frome*, and in 1921 became the first woman to win the Pulitzer Prize, for her novel *The Age of Innocence*.

The Age of Innocence (1920) is an accurate portrayal of the New York society that Wharton grew up in and was therefore familiar with, and her characters' struggle to decide between duty and passion is touchingly described. It became, as Wharton herself said, 'one of my rare best-sellers!' An Oscar-winning film of the story, starring Daniel Day-Lewis and Michelle Pfeiffer, was made in 1993 by the director Martin Scorsese, and is considered by some to be his best work.

OXFORD BOOKWORMS LIBRARY

Classics • Crime & Mystery • Factfiles • Fantasy & Horror
Human Interest • Playscripts • Thriller & Adventure
True Stories • World Stories

The OXFORD BOOKWORMS LIBRARY provides enjoyable reading in English, with a wide range of classic and modern fiction, non-fiction, and plays. It includes original and adapted texts in seven carefully graded language stages, which take learners from beginner to advanced level. An overview is given on the next pages.

All Stage 1 titles are available as audio recordings, as well as over eighty other titles from Starter to Stage 6. All Starters and many titles at Stages 1 to 4 are specially recommended for younger learners. Every Bookworm is illustrated, and Starters and Factfiles have full-colour illustrations.

The OXFORD BOOKWORMS LIBRARY also offers extensive support. Each book contains an introduction to the story, notes about the author, a glossary, and activities. Additional resources include tests and worksheets, and answers for these and for the activities in the books. There is advice on running a class library, using audio recordings, and the many ways of using Oxford Bookworms in reading programmes. Resource materials are available on the website <www.oup.com/elt/bookworms>.

The *Oxford Bookworms Collection* is a series for advanced learners. It consists of volumes of short stories by well-known authors, both classic and modern. Texts are not abridged or adapted in any way, but carefully selected to be accessible to the advanced student.

You can find details and a full list of titles in the *Oxford Bookworms Library Catalogue* and *Oxford English Language Teaching Catalogues*, and on the website <www.oup.com/elt/bookworms>.

THE OXFORD BOOKWORMS LIBRARY
GRADING AND SAMPLE EXTRACTS

STARTER • 250 HEADWORDS

present simple – present continuous – imperative –
can/*cannot*, *must* – *going to* (future) – simple gerunds …

Her phone is ringing – but where is it?

Sally gets out of bed and looks in her bag. No phone. She looks under the bed. No phone. Then she looks behind the door. There is her phone. Sally picks up her phone and answers it. *Sally's Phone*

STAGE 1 • 400 HEADWORDS

… past simple – coordination with *and*, *but*, *or* –
subordination with *before*, *after*, *when*, *because*, *so* …

I knew him in Persia. He was a famous builder and I worked with him there. For a time I was his friend, but not for long. When he came to Paris, I came after him – I wanted to watch him. He was a very clever, very dangerous man. *The Phantom of the Opera*

STAGE 2 • 700 HEADWORDS

… present perfect – *will* (future) – *(don't) have to*, *must not*, *could* –
comparison of adjectives – simple *if* clauses – past continuous –
tag questions – *ask*/*tell* + infinitive …

While I was writing these words in my diary, I decided what to do. I must try to escape. I shall try to get down the wall outside. The window is high above the ground, but I have to try. I shall take some of the gold with me – if I escape, perhaps it will be helpful later. *Dracula*

STAGE 3 • 1000 HEADWORDS

... should, may – present perfect continuous – *used to* – past perfect –
causative – relative clauses – indirect statements ...

Of course, it was most important that no one should see Colin, Mary, or Dickon entering the secret garden. So Colin gave orders to the gardeners that they must all keep away from that part of the garden in future. *The Secret Garden*

STAGE 4 • 1400 HEADWORDS

... past perfect continuous – passive (simple forms) –
would conditional clauses – indirect questions –
relatives with *where/when* – gerunds after prepositions/phrases ...

I was glad. Now Hyde could not show his face to the world again. If he did, every honest man in London would be proud to report him to the police. *Dr Jekyll and Mr Hyde*

STAGE 5 • 1800 HEADWORDS

... future continuous – future perfect –
passive (modals, continuous forms) –
would have conditional clauses – modals + perfect infinitive ...

If he had spoken Estella's name, I would have hit him. I was so angry with him, and so depressed about my future, that I could not eat the breakfast. Instead I went straight to the old house. *Great Expectations*

STAGE 6 • 2500 HEADWORDS

... passive (infinitives, gerunds) – advanced modal meanings –
clauses of concession, condition

When I stepped up to the piano, I was confident. It was as if I knew that the prodigy side of me really did exist. And when I started to play, I was so caught up in how lovely I looked that I didn't worry how I would sound. *The Joy Luck Club*